Values—Not Just for the Office Wall Plaque

HOW PERSONAL AND COMPANY VALUES INTERSECT

First published in USA by
Evolution Consulting, 2012
Dublin, Ireland

Copyright © 2012 Irial O'Farrell

Printed in USA by Create Space, Charleston, South Carolina, USA

ISBN-10: 1461058368

ISBN-13: 9781461058366

Values—Not Just for the Office Wall Plaque

HOW PERSONAL AND COMPANY VALUES INTERSECT

IRIAL O'FARRELL

Evolution Consulting
Dublin, Ireland

To Keith, for his enduring support and belief in me

Contents

Preface

Along with reading books, I've always enjoyed the process of writing. Over the course of my career as a training manager, I was able to indulge my interest through preparing course manuals required to accompany training interventions I designed and delivered. However, when I moved away from regular training and set up my own coaching and consultancy business in 2006, writing opportunities were few and far between.

I suppose one could say that my need to write became a bit of an itch that I needed to scratch, which gradually intensified over the next few years, culminating, in around 2009, in my idea to write a book. So, I started playing around with suitable topics, mainly related to my professional experience. Subjects such as performance management, management skills, and effective leadership sprung to mind but none of them really grabbed me as a first book.

While I hadn't quite settled on the book's theme, over the course of the next couple of years, I researched writing and book publishing by attending a writing course, contacting some publishers, learning about the book publishing process, and writing several blogs and articles. I kept chipping away at it.

Then, in early 2011, it hit me. My book would be about values, what they are, how they work, on both an individual and organizational level, and how they can help a business improve its performance. I had been fascinated by the topic since I first came across personal values as part of my executive coaching course in 2006. My own learning and insights into how my values had unwittingly been influencing me were a real eye-opener and helped me better understand the causes of repeat patterns and conflicts in my life.

What I noticed while working with clients was that they similarly gained huge benefits from understanding what values are, how they work, and what their own personal values were. They gained huge relief from clearly being aware of the differences in values and that one set of values isn't any better or worse than another set, just different. They also gained a better handle on the source of conflicts and were able to de-personalize situations that previously had been eating them up. The bottom line was that when employees understood their own values, their performance in the workplace became more effective.

Working with individual employees or teams within companies led me into the area of values in an organizational context. Working with one employee on his or her values is relatively straightforward; but how do values work when there are two hundred or two thousand employees involved? After all, many companies happily state a set of core values, get a nice plaque made, put it up on the wall, and then never look at it again, possibly because they don't know what to do next. Time and again, I've heard people comment about how they don't understand how a specific action taken by their manager, or their organization as a whole, fits in with their company's value of integrity or respect or whatever the value *du jour* is.

So I started to work with businesses to help them understand what company values are, how they can work at a company-wide level, and how they need to be rolled out and supported to be effectively implemented. After years of honing my theories and observations, through practical application, discussion, and testing theories, by the time I had the idea to write the book on values in the workplace, the material just flowed.

I hope you enjoy it and take away some useful insights.

Acknowledgments

To all those people who allowed me to work with them and their values, be they personal or company. Without you taking a leap of faith and placing your trust in me, I would never have gathered the insights required to either understand values at such a deep level or been able to write this book.

To everyone who helped me to write and publish this book, I am very grateful. In particular, to Noel Caffrey, Mary Calpin, Dr. Dilis Clare, and David Wells, for taking the time to read the manuscript and provide honest, constructive feedback.

To Keith Farrell, for your constant support and for pointing out the obvious: "Sit down and just write it."

For everyone I conversed with during the writing of this book. Not only did your questions confirm I was covering the right material, but your curiosity led me to conclude there's a lot of interest in personal and company values but, perhaps, not so many answers available.

Introduction

Enron[1] was formed in 1985 through the merger of Houston Natural Gas and InterNorth, and its one-time mission statement was "*to become the world's leading energy company*" by upholding the values[2] of:

— *Communication*
— *Respect*
— *Integrity*
— *Excellence*

During the following fifteen years, it went on to achieve this by growing from a non-entity to America's seventh-largest company, employing twenty-one thousand staff members in more than forty countries. In October 2001, the dream shattered as a culture of deceit, special purpose entities, and questionable accounting practices was uncovered, leading to its share price sinking like a lead balloon.

What happened? How did Enron's values of integrity, respect, and excellence let it down? Surely integrity would have guided it to do the right thing and correctly account for its assets? Or respect would have guided it to be respectful of the right of its customers, staff, and shareholders to know Enron's true financial position? Or that excellence meant it valued achieving tangible performance and not a paper trail of nothingness?

---

1 Wikipedia, Enron, http://en.wikipedia.org/wiki/Enron

2 The New York Times, James S. Kunen, January 19, 2002, Enron's Vision (and Values) Thing http://www.nytimes.com/2002/01/19/opinion/enron-s-vision-and-values-thing.html

Clearly, there was a mismatch between Enron's corporate values and its actions. What caused this mismatch? Did the company as a whole really believe in these values or were they just optional aspirations that could be ignored? Did anybody believe in them or was it just the board, the chief executive officer (CEO), the chief financial officer (CFO), and the other four hundred employees that were let go in the aftermath that didn't buy into them? Were integrity, excellence, and respect just impressive-sounding words, proudly displayed on a wall plaque in the office foyer, gathering dust, while the real, unspoken company values were being actively upheld through actions and intentions?

More recently, what about the prevalent values that influenced and contributed to the global financial meltdown of 2008? In *The Big Short*, Michael Lewis describes that the culture in AIG Financial Products (AIG FP), a key player in the financial house of cards, became a dictatorship, whereby obedience and control were the required values. As Lewis tells it, anyone who questioned the boss, or his decisions, was shot down and humiliated, eventually resulting in the desired behaviors and, on the face of it, adherence with the desired values.

The impact of actively having the values of obedience and control was that nobody effectively questioned the risks AIG FP was taking on or the price at which it was taking them on. During the upswing, AIG FP was posting great returns, which made everyone happy, but, when the downswing eventually took place, AIG nearly went to the wall, narrowly escaping Enron's fate.

Company values, personal values, team values—values are mentioned everywhere these days but what exactly are they and what, if anything, is so important about them?

Over the last six years, these and many other questions about values have cropped up during my work with business owners, executive teams, leaders, managers, and human resource professionals. These people have heard the words but often have many questions about what they are and how they work in practice, particularly in relation to company values. After all, how does an organization go about aligning five, five hundred, or five thousand staff members to one set of core values?

Since I first encountered values as part of my own development as an executive coach, I've been fascinated by how powerful the understanding and use of them can be. From my own experience, awareness of my values helped me to see different perspectives and interactions more clearly. The result was that I was able to de-personalize situations and see them for what they were, rather than how I thought they should be. In turn, these insights reduced the amount of conflict I internalized and minimized the debilitating self-talk that accompanied it. I was also better able to hold my own counsel and to make decisions that were right for me, without the need to constantly question them or run them past others, as would have happened previously.

As I started to work with other people and their values, I noticed they also benefited from similar outcomes, whether they were individuals or teams. They consistently seemed calmer and happier; they were better able to de-personalize negative interactions, enabling them to engage in less conflict; and they were more confident in making the right decisions for themselves.

Another observation was that, when I worked with employees of companies that had a set of company values, they often had no engagement with them. They either didn't know what the values were or they did but had no idea what they meant. For some, they were skeptical, having seen incidents when the values were blatantly ignored by management. In effect, a company might have had a nice set of corporate values but there was no sense of living them, rendering them useless. Clearly, there was a huge gap between having a set of values displayed on the wall and their impact on daily business.

This naturally led me on to work with values and organizations, helping them understand what values are and how upholding them positively benefits their business. I have worked with many organizations that were interested in incorporating company values into their way of doing business. Working with both executive teams and business owners has led to all sorts of interesting questions around how company values should be identified, rolled out, applied, and upheld. By engaging in these conversations over the years, I've had time to consider many practical issues and concerns and how they might best be approached. I've also been privileged to see many of these ideas successfully put into action.

Who Should Read This Book?

The main focus of this book is how values, both personal and collective, demonstrate themselves in the workplace and how they impact a company's performance. As we saw in the AIG FP example, executives are hugely influential in setting the workplace culture, so executives need to be very aware of their own values and how their resultant actions impact the business. Therefore, this book is very relevant to all executives within an organization, be it for-profit or not-for-profit, particularly CEOs, small-business owners, and heads of functions, along with all levels of management.

Understanding the concept of values is also highly relevant to anyone involved in developing and changing an organization's culture, such as organizational design consultants, executive coaches, human resources and talent management specialists, learning and development practitioners, and management consultants.

Given that this book looks at personal values and how they intersect with a company's core values, it also provides insights for any employee, particularly those who find themselves in regular conflict, either internally within themselves or externally with others throughout the company.

This Book's Objectives

The objectives of the book are to explain what values are, why they matter to a company, and how they can be identified and successfully implemented. Some of the questions that will be answered are:

— *What are personal values?*
— *What are company values?*
— *Why bother with company values?*
— *How do values—personal and company—work?*
— *How do personal values intersect with company values?*
— *How to identify a meaningful set of company values?*
— *How to implement a set of company values?*

— *How to sustain and grow a company, without diluting values alignment?*

— *How to incorporate company values into everyday business life?*

How This Book Is Structured

This book sets out to explain what values are and how they impact a business' performance, both positively and negatively.

Each chapter expands on a theme and finishes with a summary of the main points made within that chapter.

 Key concepts are denoted by this sign and are used to highlight points that are particularly important to understand and to keep to the forefront while reading the remaining material.

 Practical guides outline a suggested approach that can be followed to apply some of the ideas in the workplace. They are denoted by a set of building blocks to indicate that implementing these ideas builds the environment and engagement required to successfully create a values-based culture.

 Recap boxes reiterate material that has already been covered and is important to recall in order to fully appreciate the current point being made.

Throughout the book, reference will be made to "employees." This includes all levels of staff, from junior staff members right up to and including the executive team.

In the interest of variety, corporate values, core values, and company values all refer to the same concept of "company values."

CHAPTER ONE

What Are Values?

Over the last ten to fifteen years, the concept of company values has become widespread. A typical process is that a company identifies anywhere between four to eight values, signs off on them, gets a nice plaque made up, and proudly hangs said plaque in the lobby, never to be looked at or considered again. They may or may not be incorporated into the company's mission statement and, of course, these days, they often make their way on to the corporate website.

Table 1.1 shows a list of typical company values. As we'll see later, the most notable thing about typical company values is how generic they are. This is a real shame because such companies miss the advantages of having unique company values and often unwittingly cause unnecessary conflict, reduced performance, and loss of credibility.

Table 1.1: Typical Company Values
Integrity
Honesty
Respect
Diversity
Commercialism
Performance or Excellence
Customer Focus
Innovation

Alongside the explosion of businesses stating company values, on an individual basis, many people who have undertaken executive coaching have become more aware of their own personal values. This has enabled them to understand and explore how their values inform their actions, perspectives, and conflicts. Table 1.2 shows a list of typical personal values[3].

Table 1.2: **Typical Personal Values**

Helpfulness
Honesty
Respect
Fairness
Punctuality
Modesty
Professionalism
Logic
Knowledge
Effectiveness
Efficiency

So, what exactly *are* values? I define personal values as follows:

KEY CONCEPT 1.1

Personal values are an internal set of standards that each of us expects ourselves, and others, to live up to. These standards are sufficiently worthwhile to us that we spend extra time and effort behaving in ways that uphold them.

---

3 For a more in-depth list of values, please go to www.irialofarrell.com.

This definition provides some powerful insights into how values can impact each of us individually and our relationships with both colleagues and the company. Before we start exploring those impacts, though, let's agree on a few ground rules of what values are and are not.

GROUND RULE 1: Everyone has values but not everyone explicitly knows what theirs are. While an individual may need help with identifying a specific value, I have yet to come across someone who cannot define or isolate a set of values. Even by listening to people talk, it is possible to pick up what is important to them.

This is a really important point as, even if some people don't explicitly know what their values are, they still have an implicit set of standards that they expect themselves, and others, to live up to. More importantly, they still act, make decisions, and see the world through the filter of their values. The complication is that they just don't know what those filters are. This point becomes even more important in a team or organizational setting, but that's for later.

KEY CONCEPT 1.2

People have personal values, even if they are not explicitly aware of them.

GROUND RULE 2: Values have nothing to do with morality. That's not to say that certain moral values haven't found their way into a person's set of values through absorbing values from those around them. It is just to say that a person's values are not intrinsically linked to morals.

GROUND RULE 3: We aren't born with values. Instead, we absorb them through osmosis, by watching those around us. We can absorb them in a positive way, by seeing someone we admire and love exhibit behaviors consistent with their own values and we imitate them. Or they may have actively held us to their values and so they became important to us. For example, a parent might hold a child to always tell the truth or to always include everyone in whatever activity is taking place. In turn, the child grows up to value honesty or inclusiveness.

Alternatively, we may develop a value as a reaction to how we see someone else behaving, e.g., if someone is always late or disorganized and we don't like the impact it has, we may start valuing "punctuality" or "preparedness."

As children, our parents (or guardians) have a huge impact on shaping our values. Through their actions and behaviors, we ascertain what they value (whether they realize it or not). If the family unit has a positive influence on a child, the child will often try to behave in ways consistent with those values. If the family unit has a negative influence, it is likely that a child may well behave in ways that rebel against them.

For example, a parent who is always out indulging in their needs and always putting themselves first might be said to value selfishness. As a child on the receiving end of such treatment, the child might determine that selfishness is the way to go and start behaving in a selfish manner. Alternately, the child might sense the destructive impact on him or her and/or on others and intuitively decide they never want to act in that way. Over time, they might start to value behaviors and actions more consistent with caring or reliability.

GROUND RULE 4: For any given person's values, there is no judgment, i.e., there isn't a "good" set of values and a "bad" set of values. They are just what individuals deem as important to them. A caveat here is that acting in accordance with one's values that lead to socially or legally unacceptable behaviors does not excuse those unacceptable behaviors. To date, I've yet to come across someone whose values have generated such conflicts but that's not to say such situations don't exist.

GROUND RULE 5: Going back to the definition of personal values, we expect ourselves to live up to our own personal values and if we fail to, it typically causes us internal conflict. The more aware we are of our own values, the easier it is to recognize that we are not honoring them. As with other choices, we can choose to honor them or dishonor them and manage the subsequent consequences but, ideally, it should be from a position of knowledge and awareness, as dishonoring a value, through lack of awareness, can cause internal conflict without understanding the source.

The less aware we are of our values, the harder it is to identify times when we are not honoring them. The result for many is that they feel internal conflict but don't understand the source of it. This can lead to unease and emotional outbursts, which are often inappropriate, especially if they take place in the workplace.

GROUND RULE 6: Adding another layer of complexity, all of us have values but not everyone's values are the same. Following this through, while in some cases our values are similar to others, in other cases they clash, leading to conflict. Let's have a look at John and Laura's values and see how they might clash.

Laura's personal values are curiosity, optimism, and reasonableness while John's are decisiveness, power, and assertiveness. As we can see, there is nothing right or wrong with either set of values; they just are what they are. Now, let's look at them in practice.

Laura's value of curiosity leads her to constantly question and wonder aloud about how a decision or a situation could turn out. In turn, this behavior might really upset or negatively impact John, as he filters these actions through his own values of decisiveness, power, and assertiveness. He might interpret these questions as undermining the decisions he has made and start seeing such ponderings as an attack on his position of power.

John will probably start to shut down Laura's questions by cutting her off, interrupting her, and moving the conversation on. In turn, Laura will start to feel she is not being listened to or that her points are not being given due consideration and she might find John's behavior unreasonable. It leads to a downward spiral and a poor relationship, underpinned by low-level tension and conflict.

Both Laura and John see the other person's outward behaviors filtered through their own personal values. Since neither of them understands the position the other is coming from, it just causes more conflict and distress. If Laura and John work together, this conflict has wider implications, such as poorer decisions being made or conflict spreading throughout the team.

GROUND RULE 7: For the final ground rule on values, let's revisit our values definition. It states that values are *"standards we expect ourselves, and others, to live up to."*

This implies that we expect both ourselves *and others* to live up to *our* values. The only problem with this is that other people are too busy expecting *themselves* and *us* to live up to *their* values to be bothered with living up to ours. Multiply this assumption by the ten, two hundred, or fifteen thousand employees in a company and we get a sense of the multiple problems that such an assumption generates.

Who's right? Who's wrong? On a personal level, there is no right or wrong, just differing sets of values. However, not being aware of and understanding the impact of this basic assumption can cause emotional distress and conflict within an employee and spill over into the wider organizational context. In turn, this diverts people's energy away from what they should be focused on, i.e., the company's objectives and purpose. This ultimately leads to lower performance than the company is capable of.

While it is, strictly speaking, correct to say that no individual person's values are more right or more wrong than any other person's values, in chapter five we'll explore this idea further in relation to the natural hierarchy that exists in organizations and what actually happens in practice.

We all have values, whether we are aware of them or not. They are a set of expectations that we have of ourselves and others. If individuals uphold their values, decisions and actions tend to flow easily. If they do not uphold them, or a person comes into contact with another person who does not uphold them, conflict will most likely arise. This negatively impacts the employee's ability to perform at his or her best, resulting in an underperformance for the company.

Chapter One Summary

— *Values are defined as a set of standards that we expect ourselves, and others, to live up to.*

— *We all have our own personal values, whether we are aware of them or not.*

— *If we uphold our values, they provide us guidance in how we behave and make decisions.*

— *Our values can bring us into conflict with people who hold differing values.*

— *Not upholding our own personal values can cause internal conflict.*

CHAPTER TWO

Identifying Personal Values

Identifying Personal Values

Before an organization can start developing appropriate company values, the starting point is for key employees to understand their own personal values. Through my experience of developing leaders, I have found that a very effective way of uncovering and defining one's personal values is by working with a professional, such as an executive coach or an organizational psychologist, who is experienced in this particular area.

While each professional has his or her own approach to uncover a client's values, I take a two-pronged approach, which is explained below. I will also outline a third method that some people might find beneficial. For a reader who isn't actively aware of their own personal values, it might be useful to work through one of these methods to uncover them.

Two-Pronged Approach Explained

When working on values with clients, I have found that they often don't know what values are or how to identify their own. So, I devised what I call the "two-pronged approach" to help them understand the concept and how they can pinpoint theirs.

The first prong is to outline what I consider the "positive approach," i.e., I explain to the client that values are things that we feel are worth going the extra mile for, ideas or actions that we put extra time into because we see them as very important (or "of value") to us.

The second prong is to outline what I consider the "negative approach," i.e., I explain that values often show up when we come into conflict with others, that often the cause of the conflict is that our values have been trampled on.

I then ask the client to use either approach to help them identify some of their personal values. By explaining the process of identifying values from both a positive and negative perceptive, I have found that most people naturally select the route most applicable to them and they use it to tease out their own values.

Method 1: The Positive Approach

Where this route has been selected, I ask the person to look at their behaviors and actions and identify areas that, on pain of death, they would want to continue with. For example, a client might identify actions such as writing thank-you cards, holding doors open for people, or always being on time.

Using the process outlined in Practical Guide 2.1, I ask the client to list all behaviors and actions that are important to them, while I note them down. Looking for themes, I make suggestions as to what their values might be. If a value name resonates with them, I move on to the next value.

If the suggested name doesn't resonate with them, we explore what doesn't sit right with them about it, which word would better describe the value, and if there are any additional words and actions missing from the list that better reflect it.

This is then repeated until we have identified the client's core values. I find it worth taking some extra time to tease out what each one means in more detail (step 5). This often throws out additional descriptions of what they associate with a given value.

Practical Guide 2.1

METHOD 1: POSITIVE APPROACH

Step 1: List behaviors and actions that are important to the individual.

Step 2: Sort list into groups.

Step 3: For each group, determine a word that links all the words together. This is the value name for that group.

Step 4: Repeat until each group has been named.

Step 5: For each value, identify any additional behaviors or actions that are relevant.

Identifying Values—Positive Approach Example

Randy identified the following list of actions and behaviors, in no particular order, that he recognized were important to him:

> Asks questions; loves gizmos and gadgets; makes sure everyone gets the same chance; considers the fairest way to do something for everyone involved; lets others finish their sentences; asks people to do things in a nice, calm tone of voice; no shouting or yelling; spends time figuring out how things work together; likes trying out new things; loves hearing about new ideas; opens the door for others; arrives on time; divides things out evenly (regardless of need); likes to keep others in the loop

As we looked at the list in more detail, we sorted them into the following three groups:

Group 1: asks questions; spends time figuring out how things work together; likes trying out new things; loves hearing about new ideas; loves gizmos and gadgets

Group 2: always makes sure everyone gets the same chance; divides things out evenly (regardless of need); considers the fairest way to do something for everyone involved

Group 3: lets others finish their sentences; holds the door open for others; arrives on time; keeps others in the loop; no shouting or yelling; asks people to do things in a nice, calm tone of voice

Examining the collective behaviors and interests of each group, I suggested to Randy that group 1 represented a value of curiosity while group 2 represented fairness and group 3 represented respect. I then confirmed if these felt right to Randy. In his case, they did, but if they hadn't, I would have asked him more questions to help him tease out further what he meant by the behaviors and continued until he had isolated the most appropriate names for them.

Method 2: The Negative Approach

In situations where this route has been selected, as outlined in Practical Guide 2.2, I ask the client to identify a recent incident or situation that irked or upset them, or, alternatively, a specific person who just generally annoys them. I then ask them to pinpoint what specific behaviors, actions, or words cause the heckles to rise on the back of their neck.

Finally, I ask them to consider how they are interpreting this information. For example, do they see it as being disrespectful, distrusting, rude, arrogant, or tedious? Or do they see it as pedantic, ineffective, undermining, boring, or too risky?

In my experience, the identified behaviors tend to be ones that are in conflict with the client's own values and this is what causes the conflict. Going back to our definition of values, the client's expectations of themselves and others are not being met and this is causing the upset.

Again, once a value has been named, I ensure it resonates with the client. If it doesn't, we continue exploring and suggesting names until we identify the correct value.

As with the positive approach above, once the core values have been named, it's important to work with the client to identify further behaviors and actions that they associate with each one.

Practical Guide 2.2

METHOD 2: NEGATIVE APPROACH

Step 1: Identify a recent incident that upset the individual or caused conflict.

Step 2: Describe what was it about the incident that caused the upset or conflict.

Step 3: Name the value that was being trampled on (see suggested questions below) and validate with client.

Step 4: Repeat Steps 1 to 3 until several values have been identified and named.

Step 5: For each value, identify any additional behaviors or actions that are relevant.

Identifying Values—Negative Approach Example

Kate's boss was constantly asking for updates. He always wanted to know what was going on, he regularly looked at the details, and he questioned the approaches and methods used. This drove Kate to distraction. To her, it was meddlesome and unnecessary. It made her feel like nothing she did was believed in or accepted. In fact, the more Kate thought about it, the more it felt like her work wasn't trusted.

As it turned out, Kate valued trust, and part of her definition of trust was that if someone gave a status update or provided data, it should be accepted. In Kate's eyes, to question the information she provided was to question her trustworthiness.

When using this approach, some questions that can be useful to draw out underlying reasons for the upset or conflict are:

— *What is it about that behavior that is upsetting or annoying?*
— *What about that behavior upsets them so much?*
— *Why does that behavior matter so much to them?*
— *If the other person behaved in a different way, would they feel differently?*

By noting down the behaviors and thoughts identified, this information can then be used to isolate the value that is being violated.

Kate's answers were as follows:

— *The constant questioning and never seeming to accept what I tell him*
— *It feels like he has to double-check all my work to make sure I'm telling the truth.*
— *I feel he doesn't trust me or my work.*
— *If he took my word for it, everything would be fine. He never even finds anything wrong.*

Due to Kate's value of trust, she was filtering her boss's actions through her expectations. She was comparing his actions to her interpretation of "trustworthy behaviors." Since they didn't match, she concluded that her boss didn't trust her work and this really rankled her.

By exploring the conflict and understanding the underlying causes of it, Kate was able to pinpoint that she values trust.

Method 3: Ranking a List of Values

A third route to determining a person's values, as outlined in Practical Guide 2.3, is to ask the individual to look at a list of values and to pick out some that really resonate with them. They can select up to twenty values that they connect with.

They then need to rank them as they see fit, from most important to least important. So, if they select ten values, they should assign each one a unique number from one to ten, with one being the most important to them and ten being the least important[4].

Practical Guide 2.3

METHOD 3: RANKING VALUES

Step 1: Review a list of values and select 10 to 20 that resonate.

Step 2: Rank each value, with 1 being most important.

Step 3: Select the top 5 or 6 values. These are the core values.

Step 4: List behaviors and actions that are associated with each value.

Next, they take the top five to six ranked values and confirm that they really do represent the most important values to them. In effect, these are the individual's personal values. Once finalized, they should take the time to describe the behaviors and actions they feel would uphold each of these values.

---

4 See www.irialofarrell.com for a comprehensive list of values that can be used for this exercise.

Method 3—A Word of Caution

While method 3 is a valid way to identify values, seeing a long list of values, i.e., what's on the menu, can influence and/or narrow a person's selection, thus preventing a true reflection of what an individual really does value.

An example of this is someone who values "avoiding conflict," which will be discussed in more detail later. Part of the definition of values includes the idea that *these standards are sufficiently worthwhile that we spend extra time and effort behaving in ways that uphold them.* So, if a person puts a lot of time and effort moving away from and avoiding conflict, they actually value avoiding conflict and they actively hold an internal set of standards around not getting into conflict situations. Using a list of values would miss such a value, as it isn't one that is typically highlighted.

Validating Personal Values

Regardless of which method (or methods) is used to identify values, it's important that an employee takes a moment to consider if they feel connected to them or if they feel that something is missing. If they don't feel right, it could be that they haven't uncovered enough of the story to get to the heart of a value.

Once a set of personal values has been settled on, it is important to take time to explore each one in more detail. While specific behaviors, preferences, and actions have already been isolated to describe and support each value, is there a wider context to consider?

Following on from Randy's example, let's take a further look at respect, which Randy initially defined as:

Group 3—Respect: lets others finish their sentences; holds the door open for others; arrives on time; keeps others in the loop; no shouting or yelling; asks people to do things in a nice, calm tone of voice.

In addition to this definition, are there other behaviors that Randy sees as respectful? How would he honor respect in specific situations? How would he want to uphold respect when someone is being rude to him? Or how does he want to honor respect during times of frustration or conflict? Or when other people's views differ to his? Does he continue to listen or does he switch off? If he switches off, is that "respectful"?

This step in the process is "kick the tires" time—it involves really exploring what a value means during the tough, as well as the good, times. As with most things, it's easy to uphold values when everything is plain sailing. It's in times of tough decisions and crises that our dedication to upholding them becomes difficult and comes under the spotlight.

Once the tires were suitably kicked, Randy's final definition of respect looked something like this:

Respect: lets others finish their sentences; holds the door open for others; arrives on time; keeps others in the loop; no shouting or yelling; asks people to do things in a nice, calm tone of voice; maintains composure; keeps to the point and doesn't ramble; listens to what someone is actually saying and not drifting off; considers other people's needs; asks questions to understand where they are coming from; seeks to find win-win solutions in all situations, especially during times of conflict; maintains own standard of respect, even when someone is behaving inappropriately.

By taking the time to further explore what each value means to the employee, it provides a conscious understanding of what their values are, how they specifically interpret each one, and the behaviors they deem to be consistent with them.

Reasons to Understand Personal Definition of a Value

Why is it necessary for an individual to understand their own interpretation of a value? Doesn't everyone who values trust define it in the same way? Well, not necessarily. Let's look at the following example:

Brenda defines fairness as:

> **Fairness:** Always makes sure everyone gets the same chance; divides things out evenly (regardless of need); considers the fairest way to do something for everyone involved

Paul also values fairness and he defines it as follows:

> **Fairness:** Asking for and allowing everyone to give their contribution but having the final say; determining who

needs what and dividing resources accordingly; encouraging and enabling everyone to participate

Both Brenda and Paul value fairness but, as always, the devil is in the detail and their definitions aren't the same. Not only that, their different interpretations might actually lead to conflict, even though they share the same value.

Paul sees it as fair to ask for input but to not necessarily take all of it into account when making decisions. He also looks at individual needs and divides resources out as per need, not as per the number of people involved. Brenda sees fairness in such a way that she divides resources evenly, regardless of need.

Again, neither person is right or wrong; they are just interpreting fairness in slightly different ways. As can easily be appreciated, this difference of interpretation starts to add complexity when applied in an organizational context.

KEY CONCEPT 2.1

The need for an individual to understand their own definition of a specific value is important for the following reasons:

— *Provides a greater awareness of what the value does and doesn't mean to them.*

— *The current definition may be very narrow. Recognizing this enables their definition to be widened.*

— *As their awareness increases, the definition of the value can also expand to incorporate a wider understanding.*

— *As situations and crises arise, a benchmark is readily available to them to consider if actions, behaviors, and/ or decisions are done in a way that honors the value or not.*

Impact of Not Understanding Personal Values or Their Meanings

While numerous valid values are available, for any given person only a handful will hold any real meaning. For people who are unaware of their values, there is often a disconnect between what they genuinely value and how they actually behave.

For example, someone might genuinely value inclusiveness yet, due to circumstances or other reasons, they act very competitively. Externally, they are displaying behavior incongruent with what is really important to them, in this case inclusiveness. Unfortunately, other people read and interpret actions and behaviors, not what is said or what, deep down, might be the truth.

This can cause problems for the employee. It can cause internal conflict due to the incongruence, which can spill over into their interactions with colleagues or clients. It can also be misunderstood by others and interpreted as inconsistent behavior, potentially resulting in mistrust.

Observations on Personal Values

While working with people to uncover their personal values, I have observed several interesting trends, as listed in Table 2.1: Values Observations. Before exploring them, though, it is worth recalling the definition of personal values:

Recap

Personal values are an internal set of standards that each of us expects ourselves, and others, to live up to. These standards are sufficiently worthwhile to us that we spend extra time and effort behaving in ways that uphold them.

So, personal values are those values that an individual feels are worth going that extra mile for, over and above others. By implication, while any given individual may feel a specific value is important in a social or business sense, e.g., honesty or fairness, they may not feel it is actually important enough to them specifically to elevate it over others that they feel a greater connection with. We will return to this point while expanding on some of the observations.

Table 2.1:
Values Observations

a) *Need to Rank Values*
b) *Positional Values*
c) *Respect*
d) *Perfection*
e) *Avoiding Conflict*
f) *Honesty*
g) *Integrity*
h) *Leadership Values*
i) *Values as Weaknesses*
j) *Money*
k) *Number of Values*
l) *Upholding Values*

The following sections expand on each of the observations, as listed in Table 2.1.

a) Observations on the Need to Rank Values

Meet Bob; he values fairness, efficiency, and results. Bob was asked to deliver a project in a very short timeframe. This meant that his team was going to have to work nights and weekends for the next three months to meet the target deliverable date. As a good manager, Bob held a team meeting to explain the situation and what was being asked of them. Afterwards, Jeff, one of the team members, asked Bob for a quiet word. He explained that he had a two-week vacation booked, and paid for, during the project timeframe.

Looking at Bob's values, it's not a surprise that this situation caused a conflict for him. He clearly wanted to meet the deadline because results are important to him. However, he also recognized that it would be unfair to ask Jeff to just cancel and reschedule his "paid-up" holiday. How can Bob resolve his conflicting values?

Bob's situation highlights how a person's set of values can come into conflict with each other, in this case, fairness and results. It also raises a series of questions that anyone using values needs to answer: How do we respond when personal values come into conflict? How can we honor them both? Which value is more important?

Bob's conundrum can be eased if he ranks his values. The final step I walk clients through is to ask them to rank their personal values, in order of most important to least. I explain that, even if they are clear on what their values are, at times situations can arise that will bring two or more of them into conflict. By knowing how they rank them when they are not under pressure, it removes the need to have to make such differentiations when they're in the midst of such a situation.

If Bob is unaware of which value is more important to him, he may make the wrong decision and cause himself internal conflict and possibly unnecessary relationship damage with Jeff and the rest of the team. In contrast, if he is aware of how he ranks his values, he can use that ranking to guide him to make a decision he is satisfied with, given the conflicting needs of Jeff, the team, the company, and Bob.

As it turns out, Bob had the foresight to rank his values and he ranked them as follows:

1. Fairness
2. Efficiency
3. Results

If Bob decided to insist that Jeff stay and get the work done, he would be honoring his value of results but causing conflict with his value of fairness, which is actually more important to him.

Instead, Bob decided to honor his value of fairness while balancing his need to focus on achieving the deadline. So, he had a chat with Jeff to explore alternative ways around the dilemma and they agreed that Jeff would cancel and reschedule the vacation for after the project completion date and the company would pay the costs incurred. Everyone was happy, positive relationships were maintained, and the project was delivered on time.

As we can see from the example above, even within a set of personal values, there is a hierarchy of most important down to least important. Depending on the situation, the ranking order may change. The main point is that we can, and do, rank our values. For anyone looking to actively use their values in everyday life, it is worthwhile taking the time upfront to rank them.

b) Observations on Positional Values

Some values lend themselves very nicely to being used to justify one's own self-interest. A perfect example of such a value is fairness. Fairness is a very popular value but many people's definitions tend to fall just beyond "what is fair to me" and just short of "what is fair for others."

This is particularly prevalent in workplaces where there is a lot of "it's not fair; Johnny/that team got...I/we didn't." Such comments tend to emanate from people who value fairness, but only as it applies to them. A value defined in such terms can be considered a positional value, i.e., this is important to the employee from their perspective but they are not too bothered as to how it applies to others.

However, a true value is one that is recognized as being important enough to be upheld at all times, not just from a position of self-interest. So, when identifying personal values, it is important to determine if the definition leans towards a positional or true value.

Values that are defined in positional terms should be challenged. They should be explored to determine if they really are values, i.e., a standard to be applied consistently across the board, or if they are positional values, i.e., defined in terms of their expectations of the world but not necessarily of themselves.

Going back to fairness, if fairness really is a valid value, then the individual should be able to see situations from a wider perspective and determine what is the fairest outcome when considering everyone's needs and desires. If the individual is only interested in what is fair from their perspective, regardless of how unfair it might be to others involved, then perhaps it's time for them to change their tune.

c) Observations on Respect

Respect regularly crops up as a value, which has led me to make three distinct observations: it tends to be defined in terms of respect between two people, it tends to be very narrowly defined, and the reason why it turns up so regularly.

When an individual identifies respect, I automatically explore how self-respect fits into their idea of respect. More often than not, they have never given this element any consideration and they may be in breach of treating themselves respectfully. For someone who identifies a value of respect, it is worthwhile taking the time to consider how they would behave and act if they treated themselves with the same level of respect they have defined for treating others. In my experience, it has thrown up some very interesting dichotomies for some individuals to explore.

As with all values, it is relatively easy to remain respectful during periods of calm, but an important question to address is how they want to uphold respect during difficult situations, e.g., during a time of conflict, or when somebody is clearly being rude and disrespectful. Incorporating these answers into their definition provides a more rounded understanding of what they mean by respect and of how they expect themselves to uphold it.

The third point on respect is that it turns up quite regularly. Such frequency is very much in keeping with people's need to be seen and acknowledged as a human being. Often, particularly in the workplace, people are regularly treated in ways that make them feel unappreciated, unseen, or irrelevant—all behaviors that are at odds with respecting a person.

d) Observations on Perfection

For people who value perfection, they tend to set themselves a very high expectation of achievement, regardless of the task at hand. If they are self-aware enough, they may restrict this expectation to themselves only. If they aren't, they may well hold this high standard of expectation for others, too. On the polite end of the scale, such people are called perfectionists. On the other end of the scale, they might be referred to as control freaks or worse.

Aside from the variety of names a person valuing perfection might pick up along the way, it can also lead to underperformance, conflict, and burn-out.

On an individual basis, valuing perfection can lead to an inability to properly allocate the correct amount of time to a task or project. An excessive amount of time perfecting the final 10 percent to add .1 percent of additional value-add to the task's outcome is a waste of resources, leading to performance issues. In a wider organizational context, a manager who values perfection might browbeat the team into attaining the manager's high standards, at the cost of both de-motivating the team and wasting valuable resources to achieve a standard not actually required. As a result, the whole team starts underperforming.

Such pressure, on self and others, can lead to burn-out. For example, an individual might be driven to meet their own internal need to honor perfection but realizes it has to be on their own time. So they start working longer hours to compensate for the fact that they can't take an extra hour during the work day to complete the task to their own internal standard. Over time, this becomes unsustainable and causes burn-out, stress, and underperformance.

The final strand to this is that a person who values perfection may get very frustrated if they don't see the same standards being achieved by others. They may look around at their peers and wonder how come they get "away with" shoddy or incomplete work. This frustration can spill over into their interactions with others and may have unintended repercussions on their relationships.

For such a person, recognizing that their value of perfection is the cause of their repeat patterns is a good starting point. They can then develop a personal strategy that allows them to question to what level any given task should be completed given the timeframe, the actual required standard, the additional benefit any extra time and effort being dedicated to it would add, and the impact on those around them. They can then apply the strategy on a regular basis to help them to shift their behavioral pattern.

For example, an airline pilot clearly needs to aim for execution of the take-off and landing processes correctly and accurately 100 percent of the time. On the other hand, there is most likely some administrative tasks that would be regarded as sufficiently complete if done to a 90 or 95 percent standard. The trick for someone who values perfection is to be able to recognize and understand the difference.

e) Observations on Avoiding Conflict
The flipside of a value being something we feel is worthwhile to go the extra effort for is a value we feel is sufficiently worthwhile to *not* deal with and actually spend a lot of time and effort avoiding. So, if a person spends a lot of time and effort moving away from a specific area, it's fair to conclude that they value "avoiding it."

This insight dawned on me as I worked with a client who actually went to great lengths to not deal with conflict. John would do anything to avoid a conflict or an argument. When I suggested that he valued avoiding conflict, he readily agreed that it was something he did genuinely value and was of great importance to him. Concerned that John might not have been a one-off, and armed with knowing what to look for, I subsequently worked with several other clients who also share this value.

As previously mentioned, values are not "good" or "bad," nor are they "right" or "wrong." They are just standards that we think we, and others, should uphold and that they are important enough to put an effort into upholding. There are many people who actively turn away from situations of conflict or refuse to engage with people who enjoy a good skirmish and it may be due to them valuing avoiding conflict.

The idea that a person can value avoiding conflict is an important one within business. Many of us can think of a manager who actively avoided or withdrew from a robust discussion or refused point-blank to hold a difficult conversation. This could well be due to the manager valuing avoiding conflict. However, the ramifications for the company are huge.

For example, a manager who values avoiding conflict and has to deal with a poor performer won't hold the required conversations, allowing the poor performance to continue. This has a devastating impact on the wider team as they watch the slacker "get away" with it.

They might end up slacking off themselves or, more likely, end up having to pick up the slack, resulting in longer working hours, burn-out, and frustration. In extreme cases, good employees leave while underperformers stay, reducing the effectiveness of the team and/or department. All this because the manager values avoiding conflict and refuses to have the difficult conversations.

There are numerous other, avoidable situations that could arise from such a value. For example, someone not sharing their brilliant ideas because they see the environment as too confrontational and the company loses out; a bully getting away with unacceptable behavior because nobody will call a halt; a dog of a project wasting valuable resources because the right conversation is not being held. Clearly, these situations can arise for reasons other than one individual valuing avoiding conflict, but a key employee having such a value can cause and/or contribute to such problems.

A final point on avoiding conflict is that, if it is possible for a person to value avoiding conflict, it is most likely that there are other avoidance-based values that exist. It is something to be aware of and keep an eye out for. If an avoidance-based value is causing problems for an employee, they can create a strategy that helps to minimize them.

f) Observations on Honesty
Keeping in mind the points I made above about positional values and that an individual can agree with the need for a "general social value" but not specifically value it his- or herself, in my experience, honesty is a good example of this.

By this, I mean that we often want and demand "honesty" from our business, political, and social leaders but, in working with people's personal values, honesty doesn't crop up nearly as regularly as respect. This insight prompted me to hold discussions with several people to see what their thoughts on the topic were. We decided that it could be that people feel that a basic level of honesty should be upheld, so don't think to specifically highlight it. It could also be one of those positional values i.e., we demand it of others but aren't too hot on speaking up if we feel that doing so might lead to an adverse impact on us.

That honesty is not as widespread as we might hope or expect could also be due to society's preference for the "little white lie" told to spare "hurt feelings." There is a tendency to categorize lying into "big lies" and "small lies" and justify telling the small ones as not really mattering "that much" or "doing much harm." However, regularly not speaking up on the small stuff provides a track record and pattern of behavior that can become hard to break on the big stuff. So, a person who doesn't speak up on a significant issue, when they know they should, often justifies their behavior with excuses such as "it wouldn't have made any difference," "they wouldn't have listened to me anyway," "he didn't want to hear any objections, so what would have been the point," etc. This can undermine their credibility, particularly for those in positions of leadership.

It could well be that the result of categorizing lies means that, for many people, they expect themselves and others to not lie about the "big stuff" but recognize that the small, harmless stuff is okay. This might also contribute to the reason honesty doesn't show up as regularly as might be expected.

This was borne out by an anecdote recounted to me. A political party had done research into what people expected of their politicians and, unsurprisingly, honesty came back as top of the list. The specific politician the party had undertaken the survey for was known to be "honest and forthright." Yet it turned out people wouldn't actually vote for him because he was "too honest"!

Again, going back to the idea that values are a set of standards we expect ourselves to live up to, how does a person upholding their values behave during a conflict of interest? A person who values honesty is most likely to speak up, even if there was a personal cost to them. Such a person can truly say that they value honesty.

Two additional points of interest about honesty:

Firstly, of the people I have worked with who do value honesty, many of them tend to rank honesty quite high, i.e., telling the truth (as they see it) is a key driving factor of their behavior. Not only that, but they have very high expectations of honesty from others, at all times.

Given the points already raised above, this naturally puts them on a collision course with others and society as a whole. Many of them struggle with the conflict that arises between them and others, due either to them honestly speaking their mind or from dealing with what they perceive as dishonesty from others. Upholding their value of honesty often results in their causing trouble for themselves.

Secondly, we demand honesty of our leaders, be they business, political, religious, or societal, yet, as discussed above, for the majority of people, we apply a double-standard. We want honesty on the "big" things but don't mind a little pragmatism on the small stuff. This causes a schism in our understanding and expectations of honesty, which may go part of the way to explain why we are often disappointed with politicians and leaders.

g) Observations on Integrity

The dictionary definition of integrity is:

a. The quality of being honest and having strong moral principles
b. The state of being whole and undivided

In terms of values, integrity is often defined as "doing the right thing." Like honesty, integrity is something we demand of our political, business, societal, and religious leaders. Not surprisingly, given its close connection with honesty, again, it isn't a value that is as widespread as one might like or assume. The importance of integrity is that it is often referred to as a key ingredient for effective leadership. In reality, though, does it more often than not tend to be a positional value? For a person to really value integrity, they need to "do the right thing," even if there is a cost to them personally.

I find this particularly intriguing as integrity is one of those ubiquitous corporate values. It seems that every second set of company values includes integrity. In fact, prompted by my own value of curiosity, I decided to conduct a little research as to how common the organizational value of integrity is.

Starting with the Fortune 500 companies list[5], I identified the top forty companies. I then looked up each website and, if avail-

---

5 Fortune 500 2010 list was used, which can be found at: http://money.cnn.com/magazines/fortune/fortune500/2010/index.html

able, noted their values. As some of the websites didn't state their core values clearly enough or didn't state them at all, I managed to identify twenty[6] sets of stated values to work with. The analysis showed that 65 percent of those twenty companies had a stated value of "integrity." The analysis confirmed the proposition—that every second company, and more, does indeed state integrity as one of their values.

However, my experience of working with people's personal values, along with anecdotal evidence from people working in companies with a stated value of integrity, leads me to believe that many of these companies struggle to actively uphold integrity, Enron being a good case in point.

In theory, as with honesty, most people might like the concept of "doing the right thing" and, if given the choice, would probably agree that they want the right thing done, particularly where pillars of society, such as politicians, religious figures, and business leaders, are concerned. Theory and practice are two totally different things, though and the right thing often doesn't happen. After all, how many people actively "do the right thing," even at a personal cost to themselves?

In the business world, not only is integrity often lacking but in instances when a person is actually trying to do the right thing, they can be thwarted by people who don't want to hear the message due to a vested interest. Some will continue the fight but many will, understandably, just let it go at that stage.

Take, for example, the bank fraud executed by John Rusnak, the former currency trader at Allfirst Bank. While there is no evidence that he defrauded the bank for his own gains, other than to hide his losses and protect both his remuneration and reputation, he did expose the company to losses of $691 million, and acted in a way that could hardly be described as upholding integrity.

As part of the external investigation conducted by Mr. Eugene Ludwig[7] on behalf of AIB, Allfirst's parent company, one of the findings was that Rusnak *"was somehow able to bully or cajole*

---

6 For statistic buffs, I recognize that this is a small sample but the results are illuminating nonetheless.

7 Ludwig Report, pages 15 and 17, is available from AIB Group website. For full website address, see Works Cited

the operations staffer responsible for confirming Mr. Rusnak's trades into not confirming all of them." In addition, from time to time, Allfirst's internal audit and risk units raised serious control issues. One highlighted risk focused on price manipulation, which was duly escalated all the way up to Allfirst's treasurer. This one risk alone was permitted to take fourteen months to be resolved, even though it was repeatedly highlighted. This is a perfect example of how an employee did speak up and rightly expressed their concerns, only to be ignored while the wrong thing prevailed.

h) Observations on Leadership Values—Honesty and Integrity

Anyone who has any understanding of what makes an effective leader will know that two values widely held up as key are honesty and integrity. Acting with honesty and integrity has a huge impact on inspiring trust, both within and outside an organization. Without trust, a company becomes paralyzed; everything becomes more difficult and time-consuming. Asking someone to do a task becomes an effort, as they are suspicious of the underlying motives. When trust exists, the impossible becomes possible. Yet, as suggested above and experience tells us time and again, honesty and integrity are not as widely valued as is expected. In light of this, a key question for any organization is: how can effective leaders be developed if they don't personally value honesty and integrity?

The answer may lie in the idea that, while a specific leader might not actually value honesty and/or integrity, he or she can still grasp the ramifications of behaving in the absence of such values. Therefore, they can see the need for the organization's leaders to actively uphold the related behaviors. So, while they might not have personally identified honesty and integrity, most people do have some sort of grasp of the related behaviors. Exploring both the positive impacts of upholding them and negative ramifications of not upholding them, and the related behaviors and expectations, can form a key part of a leader's development.

For example, I worked with one client who didn't specifically identify honesty or integrity among their values. However, during my time working with him, I watched as he acted with great integrity, for the greater good of his organization. I also watched as he led his peers into engaging in more open and honest conversations, which resulted in positive ripple effects throughout the organization.

i) Observations on Values as Weaknesses

As with anything, too much of a good thing can become a weakness. A value that is overdeveloped, at the expense of others, can blind the person and result in a strength moving along the spectrum toward a weakness.

As we saw with honesty, it is a necessary value for an effective leader. However, for someone who is so driven by *their* need to tell the truth, as they see it, they may become a loose cannon and can't be relied on during times when tact is required. They might also isolate themselves, as people start avoiding home truths they may not want to hear. The leader's value of honesty has become a driver of their actions and is negatively impacting their performance, turning it into a liability.

Similarly with perfection, someone who has excessively high standards in relation to themselves and others might start moving toward the spectrum of control, i.e., wanting things done their way because they see it as the best standard or approach. Figure 2.1 illustrates some possible value spectrums.

Figure 2.1: Illustration of Values Spectrums

Honesty	Bluntness
Perfection	Control
Safety	Risk Aversion

While values do need to be ranked, as with everything, it is important to ensure that some level of balance is maintained while upholding values and that no one value consistently dominates the others.

For an individual who recognizes that their number-one ranked value is an excessive driver for them and is causing problems, they could spend some time exploring the negative ramifications of upholding it and determine if they are greater than their need to uphold it. If the negative is outweighing the positive, it might be time to rebalance the values and find strategies to minimize the painful impact of the driver value.

j) Observations on Money:

In business, money is often thrown at problems and is regularly used as a motivating factor. How many times has a project gone out of control and the response was to throw more people and money at it? Some progress might initially be made but if the underlying causes, such as planning, clarity around goals and objectives, and roles and responsibilities, aren't dealt with, the issues inevitably raise their heads again and the project ends up back at square one.

Or how many times has money being thrown at a person threatening to walk? The pay raise might work in the short term but, again, if the underlying issues aren't dealt with, they just come back to haunt and it's often just a matter of time before the person does actually walk.

Over the years, I have facilitated numerous, often heated, discussions about whether money is a motivator, a de-motivator, or an enabler, and whether it is actual physical money that people want or what the money represents to them. While there has never been any final agreement, clearly money is necessary but do people actually "value" money? In my experience, I have yet to work with someone who identifies money as a value but that's not to say that such a value doesn't exist.

Again, since values don't carry a "right" or "wrong" tag, some people may well value money for its own inherent value. By valuing money, I mean that if it came down to a direct decision between making some money or destroying a relationship, for example, a person who values money would choose the opportunity to make the money at the expense of the relationship.

For anyone who has experienced such a situation and came out the wrong side of it, it's worth remembering that many people aren't explicitly aware of their values and often act in ways that are not in keeping with what they really value. So, at times when they had to make such a decision between money and relationships, they might have made the wrong decision, as per their values, and put the money first. Such decisions might well have caused a lot of unexplained angst for them and they might have lived to regret it. Alternatively, if the person sees money as a tool to display a value such as power, they might have made the decision based on upholding that value, rather than specifically for the money.

Since money is such a sensitive subject that impacts everyone's life, it is important to recognize that money does play a valid role. For a further discussion on that role, please see appendix A.

k) Observations on Number of Values:

When I first began exploring my own values, I had about twenty of them. After a few weeks, I realized that many were sub-sets of each other. For example, fairness and honesty might actually roll up into an overall value of integrity. While it's fun for a person to explore their personal values, if there are more than five to six, it is worth considering if some of them naturally roll up under others.

There is no ideal number of values but, in working with clients, the number of core values does tend to settle somewhere around the five mark. Trying to uphold too many more than this can start becoming counter-productive. That said, some people may have secondary values that become important if all the requirements of the core values are met.

l) Observations on Inconsistently Upholding Personal Values

I'm going to finish off this chapter with one final question to consider:

Is it possible to behave inconsistently with our values?

The short answer is yes, it is very easy to behave inconsistently with personal values. The most common causes are: (1) the person is not clearly aware of their values and/or (2) there are other, deep-seated issues driving an individual's actions.

The less aware a person is about their values, the more likely they are to behave inconsistently with them. In addition, other people develop impressions and make assumptions about us based on actions, not intentions. In effect, others might conclude that a person has values that are at odds with the person's true set of values.

While recognizing that values aren't inherently right or wrong, in my experience of working with people and their values, they usually identify values that could be considered "honorable" or "positive," such as respect, friendliness, helpfulness, or efficiency. In practice, many people behave in ways that are more consistent with values that could be considered less desirable, such as control, selfishness, competitiveness, or perfection. Such behavior is then interpreted by others as representative of what is really important to the individual. This generates an incongruence between what the individual sees themself as valuing deep down and what they exhibit to others.

When taking the time to identify personal values, it is important for the person to be very honest with themselves and uncover what they really do value and the behaviors that they feel uphold them. A comparison to their external behaviors can then highlight any incongruence[8].

The result of an employee behaving inconsistently with their values has ramifications for them, both as an individual and for their performance within the workplace, as we will see over the next two chapters. The more senior the employee, the higher the impact is within the workplace.

---

8 It is possible that an employee could have some deep-seated issue, such as low self-esteem, beliefs, or negative thought loops, that are contributing to the person behaving inconsistently with their values. Working with a professional, such as an executive coach, could uncover such issues and allow the person to behave more consistently.

Chapter Two Summary

— *Individuals need to identify and understand their own personal values.*

— *Individuals need to rank their personal values.*

— *Values can be framed in terms of what we don't want, as well as what we do want.*

— *Actively valuing honesty and integrity are not as widespread as we might assume.*

— *Even though honesty and integrity, as values, are not as widespread, leaders can still appreciate the value and importance of them and behave in ways to uphold them.*

— *Care should be taken to ensure a value doesn't become a weakness.*

— *For several reasons, we can behave inconsistently with our personal values.*

CHAPTER THREE

The Role of Company Values

Over the past decade or so, the trio of vision, mission statement, and values has become all the rage and they're still with us. Of all the business jargon and fads that come and go, values seems to be one of the more enduring, and widespread, ideas that remain with us.

What is it about values that has kept them around for so long, particularly as we can all point to incidents when companies have clearly behaved in ways inconsistent with their stated values? The usual benefits put forward to have core company values are outlined in Key Concept 3.1.

Some companies really get the point of values and, internally, they consistently live by them. The impact is that a customer or client can actually feel the values around them. They may not consciously be aware of what the values are but they pick up a general sense of consistency in the company's approach to business. The customer can then make an informed decision about whether or not they connect to and trust the company's approach. Customers that connect with it become loyal and vocal supporters of the business.

KEY CONCEPT 3.1

Typical benefits of having company values include:

— *Provide guidance as to what behavior is important in the organization*

— *Provide a decision-making framework for all employees, at all levels, in all departments*

— *Inspire employees to work toward a common way of behaving*

— *Tap into individuals' personal values, providing additional levels of motivation and connection*

— *Guide people in working toward the same goals*

— *Create a consistent customer experience that results in increased sales*

This really became apparent to me during one shopping trip. I was shopping in a multi-national furniture store. We had purchased a sofa and four sets of legs in the living room section and had continued on our merry way. A few minutes later, there was an announcement for us to return to the living room section service desk, which we did. When we got there, we were greeted by the customer service representative (CSR) on her way back from trying to find us. It turned out there was some point we had overlooked during the booking process and she wanted to make us aware of it. I was impressed by how she had gone out of her way to ensure the oversight was corrected.

When we got to the cashier section, which was a substantial distance from where we had ordered the sofa, I realized that we didn't need as many sets of legs as we had originally bought. Knowing myself well enough to know that I'd never bring them back once we left the store, I wanted to cancel one set there and then, so I went to a customer service station.

The CSR there was already "helping" a couple, so I stood to the side and watched the interaction. His manner was cross, unhelpful, and angry and, as an external party to the interaction, it really jarred with my sense of what the store was about. One unhappy customer later, it was my turn and, needless to say, I wasn't any more successful. He refused to try to cancel the set of legs on his computer, wouldn't call the order desk to ask them to cancel it, and his only solution was for me to go to the section and do it myself.

His suggestion didn't sit very well with me. Aside from the fact that I'd rather have canceled the whole order than go back upstairs, it just seemed so out of place with my experience of the store in general. Instead, I went up to the cash register and explained the situation to that CSR. Without prompting, she called up to the living room section and had the whole thing sorted in a minute, just like the other CSR could have done if he'd wanted.

While the second CSR didn't cover himself in glory, what struck me was how completely inconsistent his approach was, as compared to his colleagues'. I could sense that most staff members were quite prepared to go out of their way to help me and, not only that but it seemed that this was important to them. This is a really good example of how a company and its staff live up to their company's values. It also highlights how jarring it can be for the customer if they aren't upheld.

This story highlights two interesting points about values:

1. When a company consistently lives by its values, customers or clients sense that experience, even if they don't specifically know what the values are. This results in building trust. If they are in tune with those values and the related experience, customers will continue to engage with the company through repeat business and/or word of mouth. And, let's face it, that's the holy grail of commercial business.

2. If a company is consistently living up to its values and an employee somewhere, at whatever level within the organization, behaves inconsistently, it jars with those around them, be they customers, staff, peers, managers, or suppliers.

It just stands out and feels wrong, resulting in a certain amount of conflict.

When applied consistently, values can enhance a customer's experience and ultimately contribute to achieving a company's objectives and boosting its bottom line. Since some companies embody this so well, it is most likely a contributory factor as to why the concept of corporate values endures.

That said, as we saw with personal values, when company values are applied inconsistently, or awareness of them is totally absent, they can contribute to conflict and an inconsistent customer experience. For example, Mary and Rick, along with their twenty-two-month-old daughter, went to what was billed as a family-friendly hotel. While the hotel had facilities such as a playground, a playroom, and a children's menu, Mary and Rick's experience of getting food when they needed it for their daughter turned the experience into a nightmare. The staff allowed no flexibility for a child that needed to eat outside the times the hotel had determined, even to the point of refusing them room service.

This incident highlights how organizations use values as a marketing tool without any consideration for how they will deliver the message on a daily basis. In this case, the hotel seemed to think that providing an outdoor playground and an indoor playroom was enough to market themselves as "family friendly." They failed to take the concept of "family friendly" into the nitty-gritty of designing their facilities and services by considering what different age groups would need. In addition, they were so driven by their own internal organizational needs that they didn't allow staff any discretion or flexibility to meet individual family needs.

The gap that then arises between customers' expectations from the marketing blurb and their actual experience causes unnecessary conflict between the business and their customers, resulting in stress for both the customer and staff, reputational damage, and, ultimately, reducing the bottom line.

As most, if not all, companies experience and deal with conflict in some shape or form, the issue of values and conflict is worth exploring further, which we will do in detail in the next chapter.

Connecting Values to Vision and Mission Statement

If values can underpin a company's ability to achieve its objectives, let's take a look at how values work in tandem with an organization's vision and mission statement.

Company Vision

Typically, a company's vision is the CEO's idea of where the company is going and what it can achieve in the future. To create a vision, the CEO needs to:

1. Understand the purpose of the company. All companies are set up to make money. So what? The CEO needs to understand what makes this company so special, as compared to its competitors. Put another way, what difference would it make if this company no longer existed? Would it just be one less service/product provider or would there be a discernable gap in the lives of its customers/clients?

2. Be able to look up and out and take time to assess where the industry has come from, sense where it is going, identify what trends are occurring in the marketplace, see possible opportunities, and implement ways the business can capitalize on them.

3. Take a long, hard, honest look internally to see where the company currently is, assess what its strengths and weaknesses are, identify what needs to change, and clearly understand how those changes will contribute to the company's overall success in fulfilling its purpose.

An effective vision is one that others—the executive team, management, and staff—can connect with and buy into. As a result, the most successful visions tend to be ones that reach beyond the CEO's personal interests and needs. As a general rule, people don't tend to get too enthusiastic for a project or vision that is only self-serving for those at the top or is only concerned with maximizing the bottom line.

The following story, reproduced with kind permission from Carmine Gallo of Gallo Communications[9], is a great example of the difference between a humdrum "vision" and one that inspires:

> During my research on Steve Jobs, I interviewed Rob Campbell, the CEO of Voalte, a wireless software provider for hospitals and point-of-care facilities. In 1977, Campbell was a young programmer who was excited about the emerging class of personal computers. He began searching for a position at one of the companies at the forefront of the revolution.
>
> Campbell first visited Tandy Computers. "What is your vision for the personal computer?" he asked. "We think it could be the next big thing on everyone's wish list for the holiday session!" Tandy executives exclaimed. Uninspired, Campbell visited Commodore, a company that introduced a personal computer in 1977. Commodore's stock was trading at less than one dollar a share. "What is your vision for the personal computer?" Campbell asked. "We think it could help our stock rise above two dollars a share," Commodore executives said excitedly. Uninspired, Campbell decided to take Steve Jobs up on an invitation to meet for lunch.
>
> "What is your vision for the personal computer?" Campbell asked Jobs. Campbell said what happened next still gives him goosebumps. "Steve Jobs was a magical storyteller," Campbell told me. "For the next hour, he talked about how personal computers were going to change the world. He painted a picture of how it would change everything about the way we worked, educated our children, and entertained ourselves. You couldn't help but buy in." Vision, said Campbell, was the one thing that separated Steve Jobs from the others.

---

9 Carmine Gallo, www.carminegallo.com or www.gallocommunications.com

This is a vision that inspires—it draws people in, they can relate to and believe in it, and, most importantly, people want to be part of creating that future. That's what a truly inspiring vision does.

As this story also nicely illustrates, people are not drawn to or inspired by wishy-washy visions or visions driven by money alone. They want to be involved in something that makes a difference, that inspires them, and/or that they can connect to. That doesn't mean the vision can't turn a buck at the same time. Clearly it has to make money or the business won't last long, but it can't be all about the bottom line, either.

Let's consider the following vision a CEO has for his pharmaceutical company. His story is that while the pharmaceutical industry has made huge strides in finding solutions to many illnesses and has made a huge difference in people's lives, such as increasing the life expectancy of those with cancer and reducing cholesterol, many drugs also carry severe side effects that negatively impact the patient's quality of life. He has personally visited hospitals where patients have been too weak to move after a course of treatment and has seen the toll this has on both the patient and their families.

This CEO feels that through innovative R&D, alternative solutions can be found that balance the effectiveness of some of these drugs while minimizing the side effects, thus enhancing the quality of these patients' lives and those around them.

Again, this vision is tangible and personal. It personalizes the impact the drug company's products have on patients' lives, both the positive and negative. It makes people feel good that they have been part of something that has made such a positive impact on patients' lives while also recognizing the opportunity to make improvements by being part of creating the next generation of solutions. It also goes beyond the bottom line and connects employees to the purpose of making a tangible improvement in patients' lives.

Mission Statement and Company Values

Once the CEO has verbalized the vision, the next step is to immortalize it in a mission statement. While not all mission statements do so, best practice indicates that an effective mission statement is made up of two elements: a statement of the organization's purpose (i.e., what are we here for?) and the way in which the company proposes to achieve that purpose (i.e., the "how" they are going to go about achieving it, otherwise known as company values).

Following on from the pharmaceutical company's vision above, their mission statement is as follows:

To deliver products and solutions that enhance our customers' quality of life. We do this through focusing on innovation, reliability, and empathy.

Examining this mission statement, we can see it is made up of two parts. The first part is the purpose: to deliver products and solutions that enhance our customers' quality of life. The second part focuses on "how" this will be delivered: through innovation, reliability, and empathy.

While the second part specifically outlines how this company is going to deliver on the purpose, it's important to recognize that any number of values, and combinations, could deliver on this purpose. For this corporation, the CEO and executive team identified the importance of innovation, reliability, and empathy as the cornerstones of how they are going to achieve their purpose.

Another executive team might have chosen customer focus, product improvement, safety, and cost efficiency as their values— same purpose, an alternative route to achieving it. A third group might have chosen reliability, respect, and excellence as their "how." Again, same purpose, different "how."

A key point to remember is that none of these routes are right or wrong—they are just several paths to achieving the same purpose. That three different companies might select three different sets of values most likely reflects the diversity in the personal values held by the members of each of the executive teams.

It's also important to consider that the feel within each workplace will be distinct from the others due to the different sets of values. Values inform a company's culture, or "the unspoken rules of how we do things around here." So, even though all three organizations have the same purpose in this example, individuals will be drawn to the organization that is most closely aligned with their own personal values.

KEY CONCEPT 3.2

Two or more companies can have the same purpose but the manner in which they choose to achieve it, i.e., their company values, can be very different. In turn, this leads to different organizational cultures. The different sets of values reflect a combination of each executive team's personal values.

Defining Company Values

Company values indicate how the business proposes to achieve its purpose, which is a verbalization of the CEO's vision. Having looked at visions and mission statements, we're right back at values— there's just no getting away from them! Having defined personal values as an internal set of standards that each of us expects ourselves and others to live up to and are worth the effort, company values can be defined as:

KEY CONCEPT 3.3

Company values represent the company's internal set of standards it expects everyone within the organization, including the executive team, to live up to. They embody the business's approach to achieving its purpose.

Differentiation through Company Values

Implemented well, company values are what differentiate a business from its competitors. Values provide guidelines as to what is and isn't important for that business to achieve its mission statement. By having values, they automatically provide a set of standards that guide people on how they should behave, interact with others, and, through which, they should complete their daily/weekly/monthly work. They also offer direction to employees during the decision-making process.

What is not as explicitly highlighted is that values can also inform conflicts and, by understanding clashing values, conflict can be reduced or minimized within the workplace and between the company and its clients.

This is as true for a small business of five employees as it is for a large multi-national of fifty thousand. The difference lies in the challenge of guiding and engaging fifty thousand staff members in one set of company values versus five employees. This, of course, highlights one of the huge challenges of introducing and upholding values across larger organizations. How can they be constructed in such a way that they provide the necessary flexibility but are also accessible enough for people to understand how to use and honor them on an everyday basis? This will be addressed later on, when we look at how best to identify and implement company values.

Company Value Categories

Some corporations state a set of values and then actively live them. Other businesses explicitly state values and then ignore them, instead adhering to some unwritten set of values. Another set of companies don't mention values at all yet there is a clear sense of how they approach business, while other workplaces are oblivious to the concept of values yet they still have implicit values. How can these different categories of values be differentiated?

To be clear about the different categories of values, let's define them as outlined in Key Concept 3.4.

As with personal values, each company has a set of values, whether they are explicitly aware of them or not. This set of values has been defined as actual values. Some companies take the time to identify their actual values and evaluate how useful or necessary they are going forward.

Actual values that are confirmed as necessary to the business are defined as valid values while those that are deemed of no more use are defined as comfort values. Values that are identified as required for the company's future success but are currently not supported are defined as missing values. A company's final set of values, made up of valid and missing values, is defined as final stated values.

KEY CONCEPT 3.4

Actual Values: A company's set of implicit values that are actually lived, even if they are unspoken. All companies have actual values, whether they are aware of them or not.

Stated Values: A set of values that are selected, explicitly stated, and imposed, without undertaking the necessary analysis needed to understand what they should be.

Valid Values: Actual values that have been evaluated as being necessary for the company going forward.

Comfort Values: Actual values that have been identified as alive but are no longer of use to the company going forward.

Missing Value: A value identified as necessary for the company's future but is not currently active.

Final Stated Values: A company's stated set of values, constructed through careful analysis and with clear awareness of the company's needs. Final stated values are typically a combination of valid and missing values.

In contrast, a set of values that are just stated by a corporation, without it taking the time to understand what its actual values are, can be defined as stated values, Stating a set of values and getting back to work only takes a few hours but the likelihood of them being successfully supported is slim.

Taking the time to honestly appraise where the company is at is often very uncomfortable. On an individual basis, many people struggle to honestly appraise who they really are and what they are really about. It is painful for them to admit that they might not be as good as they think they are or that they are the cause of some of their own problems. So, they often blame external factors for their shortcomings.

This equally applies at the organizational level. It is just complicated by politics, differing personal values, and power plays. As highlighted in Jim Collins' book *Good to Great*, for those leaders that can get beyond the blame-and-politics reflexes and start honestly naming blockages and identifying their sources, they are on the ladder to moving their business from underperforming to realizing its potential. As is also emphasized in *Good to Great*, very few companies have actually achieved it.

However, a business that honestly goes through the process of uncovering its actual values, identifying its valid and missing values, and confirming a set of final stated values has a much higher chance of succeeding in implementing and supporting its values and reaping the related rewards, such as trust and customer loyalty.

The earlier in the business life cycle a company engages with the values process and takes steps to protect the progress made, the easier it is to sustain and benefit from their power. This actually gives small and growing businesses a competitive edge over some of the larger market participants. Technology companies, such as Apple and Google, seem to be particularly good at incorporating this in the start-up phase.

For an established business that decides to actively leverage values as part of rolling out and incorporating a new or revised mission statement, in-depth discussion about each of the values and what they mean in each department becomes critical to embedding them into people's everyday working lives. The more they are discussed, the greater the clarity around what they do and don't mean within the organization and how these meanings translate into behaviors and actions. This step is particularly important for an established company as it most likely hasn't been actively recruiting employees with personal values that underpin the new or revised values.

In conclusion, company values are a mechanism for companies to identify "how" they are going to achieve their purpose. They provide guidance to everyone within the organization as to what is expected of them, and how they should behave, interact, and make decisions.

Done poorly, introducing unsupported values can lead to conflict, confusion, misdirected energy, distrust, disloyalty (both inside and outside the organization), and underperformance.

Done well, values can powerfully guide all employees to actively contribute to developing and sustaining the company's culture. This translates into creating consistent customer experiences and interactions with the company, building trust, loyalty, ongoing support, superior performance, and strong financial returns.

Chapter Three Summary

— *A company that actively upholds its values creates a consistent client experience, which customers can then clearly connect to and support, creating a loyal client base.*

— *A company that doesn't consistently live up to a set of values generates a sense of inconsistency and low-level conflict for both customers and employees.*

— *A CEO's vision is captured in their company's mission statement, which consists of the business's purpose and values.*

— *Just having a set of stated values is not sufficient to reap the rewards that come with values. They must become part of the fabric of how the company does business.*

— *Identifying and implementing a set of final stated values takes a lot of time, effort, and dedication.*

CHAPTER FOUR

Values and Conflict

As we have already seen, there are many reasons to introduce an effective set of company values but, in my experience of working with employees and their values, by far the biggest benefit is the reduction in conflict. Conflict through values can arise in many different ways within an organization. By understanding those sources and creating strategies and development programs to lessen them, businesses can rapidly improve both employee and organizational performance, giving the company an edge over competitors.

This chapter will explore the cost of conflict to an organization, as well as the sources of conflict within an organization, and suggest strategies to lessen them.

One of the most striking and useful discoveries I made when I first started working with values was how they inform conflict. By understanding what personal values are and that everyone has their own set, it helps people appreciate many of the sources of the conflict they encounter. In turn, this allows better conflict management, leading to reduced frustration and an increase in an employee's ability to remain focused on their work and to influence others.

Cost of Conflict within an Organization
Think about the last time you were in a conflict situation—it might have been with your boss, a colleague, or a client.

Now, describe how you felt. Did you feel dread, or anger, or fear? How did your body respond? Did you get a roar of sound in your ear? Did your tummy tie itself up in knots? Or did your shoulders tense up? What self-talk ran around your head after the incident? How long did it take for the self-talk to talk itself out? A few minutes? A few hours? A few days? Has your self-talk started again just thinking about the incident? Is your body starting to react again, just recalling it? Conflict arises when an incident or event results in emotional turmoil.

Physical Impact of Conflict

Conflict has a physical impact on the human body, which can negatively impact a person's performance, both in the short and longer term. When an employee comes into conflict, either expected or unexpected, their body automatically responds with "fight or flight" instincts, i.e., are they going to stay and stand their ground or are they going to make a run for it?

Regardless of their choice, their body has already flooded with adrenaline so that, even if they do decide to flee and avoid the conflict, the adrenaline has still rushed its way through their system. One physical result is that the body draws blood away from the brain, reducing the employee's ability to think clearly. Other impacts are outlined in Key Concept 4.1.

KEY CONCEPT 4.1

Conflict situations flood the human body with adrenaline. The physical impact of adrenaline on the body includes:
— *Reduction in ability to think clearly*
— *Heart beating loudly*
— *Body feeling tense*
— *Butterflies in anticipation of conflict situation*
— *Tunnel vision, resulting in not being able to see clearly*
— *Thoughts become distant*
— *Difficulty in making decisions*
— *Respond inappropriately*

No matter how the employee chooses to respond to the conflict, the physical impact of the adrenaline wears off but the impact doesn't stop there.

If the response was to fight, the situation and conflict might have escalated through how they responded (e.g., answered back inappropriately, said things they didn't mean to say, etc.), causing damage (or further damage) to a relationship. They then have to deal with the outcome of their response as well as the internal self-talk that most people undergo after such an incident to justify their behavior.

If the response was to flee, it still results in the employee spending the next few minutes, hours, or even days engaged in their internal self-talk, justifying why they walked away. They might have also generated a situation whereby they walked away from an interaction, the upshot of which is that they have, in effect, acquiesced to something that they don't actually agree with or want to do. For example, the employee might have spotted aggressive behavior coming from a colleague and agreed to what the other person wanted, even though they didn't agree with the idea, just so they could avoid the conflict. Now, they're stuck with their decision. In this case, their performance is being hampered by agreeing to something that they know is not the right or best thing to do but they gave in because it was easier to choose the flight response.

Cost of Individual Conflict to the Organization

Whether the employee's response was to fight or flee, from the organization's perspective, the conflict is damaging and costly, as outlined in Key Concept 4.2. Deteriorating relationships, mistrust, hording information, unhelpfulness, and poor decisions are some of the many outcomes from such situations. If the source of the conflict is not dealt with, it becomes even more serious. Over time, a person living in a constant state of low-level conflict (by which I mean that slight dread of engaging with a specific person or department, enough so that the body and mind have registered it) may start exhibiting longer-term symptoms, such as:

— Loss of appetite
— Insomnia
— Fatigue
— Stress
— General decline in health due to impact of above symptoms

KEY CONCEPT 4.2

Organizational Cost of Conflict:
— *Poor decisions*
— *Deterioration in relationships*
— *Mistrust*
— *Hording information*
— *Lack of co-operation*
— *Loss of focus on job/tasks*
— *Underperformance*
— *Sick leave, short and long term*
— *Potential bullying claims*
— *Unnecessary staff turnover*
— *Loss of knowledge & skills*

Such physical signs may well result in an individual going on stress leave, long-term sick leave, or making a claim of bullying against a colleague or boss, none of which exactly enhances either the individual's or the company's performance.

Even if things don't deteriorate to such an extent, both the fight and flight responses tend to result in internal self-talk and rationalization, such as "I had to respond that way because..." The impact of this self-talk is to divert a lot of time, energy, and focus away from the employee's job at hand, again resulting in underperformance.

A further problem is the impact the self-talk has on relationships with others. Whether the employee is aware of it or not, their self-talk strongly influences their actions and behaviors toward others, leading to damaged or unproductive relationships, which hamper performance from the organization's perspective. For example, if an employee goes into a meeting expecting a fight, they will behave in a way that encourages and enables a fight to ensue, often without meaning to or with no awareness that they are strongly contributing to the situation.

Cost of Conflict Arising between Two Employees

What happens when conflict spills over into a relationship between two employees? Aside from the impacts on the individual, as outlined above, which are most likely affecting both parties, as the conflict deepens, it typically becomes personal, i.e., one or both parties start to see the other party behaving in ways to "annoy" or "get at" them.

As a result, their immediate relationship starts to deteriorate, resulting in information being withheld and completion of tasks slowing down as they start to score points off each other. Decision-making becomes impaired by a variety of reasons such as: information not being shared; one party would rather make a wrong decision than have to ask for data from the other employee; the decision is made taking the conflict into account rather than making the best decision for the team, department, or company.

It doesn't stop there, either. If the conflict occurs within the team, other team members start picking up on the tension and conflict. As a result, they start responding accordingly by taking sides, not getting tasks done, not sharing information, etc. If the conflict occurs between employees on different teams, it starts to grow legs by each party discussing the conflict or making comments to other people within their own teams. The conflict has the potential to start moving throughout the organization.

The other thing to consider is how high up this conflict is happening. If the two employees are at a junior level, it most likely will be contained within the immediate team. However, the higher up the grades the conflict occurs, the more influential the conflict becomes. The worst-case scenario is that the conflict occurs between two senior managers or executives across two different departments.

As the conflict spreads across teams and departments, the cost to the company continues to mount. Restricted information flow, poor decision-making, gossiping, and misdirected focus on the conflict rather than objectives across several employees or teams multiplies the impact of the conflict and undermines the company's performance.

Organizational Benefits of Reducing Conflict

What are the benefits if conflict is reduced and minimized in the workplace? By reducing conflict, employees are better able to remain clear-headed, engage in discussions that result in better decisions, maintain more effective relationships, and minimize time lost due to negative self-talk. Ultimately, this tends to result in less emotional leakage and more consistent, appropriate behavior, resulting in improvement in both the employee's and the organization's performance, in turn boosting the bottom line. See Key Concept 4.3 for full list of benefits.

KEY CONCEPT 4.3

Benefits of Minimizing Conflict include:

— *Clear, effective decisions*
— *Effective relationships*
— *Increased ability to influence*
— *Sharing of information*
— *Trust and co-operation*
— *Employee energy focused on work*
— *Achievement of objectives and projects*
— *Reduction in time lost due to gossiping*
— *Increased employee and team performance*

Sources of Conflict

How does conflict arise? For the most part, it arises because we either have desires that others (or ourselves) are thwarting or expectations (values) that we or others don't deliver on.

Conflict Arising from Desire

Take Jeff and his desire to get promoted. He has been given a really juicy project to deliver that, if all goes well, will most likely result in his getting promoted (i.e., achieving his desire). He maps out the project, assembles his team, and kicks it off. He runs into problems when another team refuses to play ball with him. They keep canceling meetings, disagreeing with his proposals, dragging their heels on providing required information, and any other way they can think to sabotage this project, as Jeff sees it.

The result is conflict between Jeff and the other team. Jeff's desire for a promotion prompts him to see the behavior of the other team as thwarting the likelihood of his desire turning into reality. He starts seeing their every move in terms of how they are trying to stop him from getting his promotion. Given the impact conflict has on the body, Jeff's every interaction with this group turns into a fight-or-flight situation, with the resultant negative impact on his interactions with them and, ultimately, his performance.

The reality is that if Jeff didn't connect success of this project with his own desire to be promoted, he would remain more clear-headed and seek ways to overcome the other team's clear reluctance to engage with him on the project. Ironically, being able to do this would more than likely result in a better outcome for Jeff, both in relation to the project and the promotion. This is a common, everyday occurrence of conflict arising out of a person's desire for something.

Conflict Arising from Values

In working with people and their values, I have observed that conflict also regularly occurs through a clash of values. In this case, it is due to a person's expectations of what they expect of themselves and others not being met. For example, Jeff and the other team could have actually been united in their desire to achieve the project outcomes and yet conflict might still arise. Rather than the conflict arising out of the other team seeming to thwart Jeff's desire, the source of this conflict arises from differences in Jeff's values and the team's values. Put another way, this type of conflict is due to how Jeff thinks, or expects, the project should be achieved and how the team thinks it should be achieved.

What I have noticed when working with clients is that, once they understand their own values and expectations and can recognize that the source of a conflict is due to reality not matching these expectations, they are better able to deflect the conflict and maintain their poise, lessening the negative impacts of conflict.

Due to multiple sets of personal values, conflict within an organization is naturally more complex. So, in order to minimize conflict across a company, it is important to have a clear understanding of the different sources of conflict in order to develop strategies to deal with it. Once understood, it takes determination and persistence to see them successfully implemented.

Levels of Conflict within an Organization

I have identified five levels of conflict within an organization, as outlined in Key Concept 4.4, arising out of differences in personal values or differences between personal and company values. As we will see, these conflicts might be caused by being unaware of values, not upholding values, or differences in ranking values.

KEY CONCEPT 4.4

Sources of Organizational Conflict:
— *Conflict within oneself, i.e., intrapersonal conflict*
— *Conflict between two people, i.e., interpersonal conflict*
— *Conflict within a team, i.e., intra-team conflict*
— *Conflict between two (or more) teams, i.e., inter-team conflict*
— *Organizational conflict, i.e., conflict between an individual or team and the organization's values*

1. Intrapersonal Conflict

During a night out with her female work colleagues, Carla discovered that a male staff member had been behaving very inappropriately toward several of the female staff. The women were making a joke of it, which caused Carla to probe further, as the male in question was going through the interview process for a promotion. She found out that all the women felt very uncomfortable in his company and were genuinely concerned that this would be exacerbated if he was promoted.

As a senior member of staff, Carla was concerned by this. Their unease matched with her own experience of interviewing the candidate. Unsure of what to do, she called a lawyer friend and explained the situation. His advice was to leave well enough alone—it was all hearsay, it could rebound spectacularly badly on Carla, and really, in his view, it was up to the female employees to raise their own concerns.

Carla listened to the advice and, on the face of it, it all seemed good and valid. There was nothing wrong with any of it, at least not that she could figure out. As he was the expert in legal matters, she took his advice and decided to say nothing, and the candidate got the promotion. The problem for Carla was that, even though she was the one who made the final decision, she never felt comfortable with it. In fact, she often ended up having sleepless nights, mulling over her decision, trying to understand what the cause of her unease was.

In reality, Carla valued integrity so, even though there were all the legal arguments such as nothing could be proven, it was nothing to do with her, and that she didn't have to take on the responsibility of other people's issues, none of them sat right with her. Carla was experiencing a disquiet, caused by her sensing deep down that the right thing to do was to address the issue, as part of a wider obligation to her position as a senior manager, to the organization, and to female employees.

Sensing the right thing and not behaving in accordance with it (or not honoring her sense of integrity) was causing Carla internal or intrapersonal conflict.

Intrapersonal conflict refers to conflict within an individual due to their personal values. Typically, it arises in two ways:

— *Lack of awareness of personal values*
— *Behaving inconsistently with known personal values*

a) Intrapersonal Conflict through Lack of Awareness of Personal Values

In this case, the employee is unaware of their values and, therefore, unknowingly behaves inconsistently with them. While such people don't understand or recognize the cause of their intrapersonal conflict, on some level, they are aware that such a conflict is taking place.

They might feel the conflict in some way, either through bodily sensations such as a knot in their stomach, a gut feeling, or through their head, e.g., constantly revisiting the issue in their thoughts, not being able to let go and/or having to discuss it over and over again, etc.

Since the employee is not explicitly aware of their values or that they have behaved in a way that is in conflict with them, they are not intentionally causing the conflict but they do live with the consequences. Such consequences might include reacting defensively or inappropriately to a situation or making decisions that are poor for them or for the organization.

While the conflict may have started off as an intrapersonal conflict, the resultant inappropriate reactions and decisions may negatively impact both the staff member's relationships and their effectiveness within the workplace. Thus, their internal conflict might well spill over into generating conflicts with others, directly or indirectly.

For Carla, her internal turmoil resulted in her avoiding the group of women, because every time she saw them, she felt guilty. She couldn't avoid herself but she could avoid reminding herself of the source of her guilt. As we can see, understanding one of the main sources of intrapersonal conflict and its impacts on both ourselves and our relationships highlights the need to explicitly understand our own personal values.

b) Intrapersonal Conflict through Behaving Inconsistently with Known Values

In this scenario, the employee is aware of their personal values but, for whatever reason, they are not upholding or honoring them. It may be that their values are not aligned with the boss's, the team's, or the organization's values and they feel under pressure to behave or act in a way that appeases others but is inconsistent with their own.

It could also be that the staff member knows what their values are but hasn't spent time ranking them. A situation then arises that brings two or more of these values into conflict. They don't know how to best honor them and this lack of clarity causes the conflict.

Finally, it could be that a situation has cropped up that is really testing the employee's dedication to their values. Perhaps a situation has arisen that would lead to something good happening for the individual, e.g., a great sales opportunity or a promotion, but it is at the expense of having to act against a personal value. Taking the opportunity and ignoring the value may cause intrapersonal conflict for the person.

Only the member of staff can determine if the conflict is worth the personal gain. For somebody in such a situation, one thing worth considering is the possible consequences that knowingly dishonoring their value might have on their subsequent behavior and actions. For example, would they be able to sleep at night? Would they always carry a feeling of "not deserving" the sale or promotion they got? Would that feeling cause them to react inappropriately, e.g., defensively or erratically, when any perceived hint of questioning their ability arose?

Alongside the impact of dealing with the internal struggle, this external pattern of behavior could have a detrimental impact on their credibility and reputation in the longer term. As we saw with Carla, her decision resulted in her not being able to face the women so she went to great lengths to avoid them. In effect, Carla lost relationships with several colleagues, the women were confused as to why she was no longer friendly with them, and Carla ended up living with a sense of low-level tension as she feared running into them on a daily basis.

Some tell-tale signs that an intrapersonal conflict has arisen are:

— *Constantly revisiting the issue*
— *Making a decision but still feeling bad about it*
— *Making a decision but then changing one's mind or re-examining it*
— *Knot in stomach, tension across the shoulders, or other bodily sensations*
— *Knot in stomach, or other bodily sensations, when the issue (be it behavior, action, or decision) is brought up*
— *An unreasonable refusal to discuss the issue and/or decision*

2. Interpersonal Conflict

Chris valued control while John valued flexibility. They had been asked to work together on a new project, having never worked together before. Chris liked to honor control by making all the decisions and by knowing what was going on at all times. At the start of each project, he liked to map out a plan, with all the steps outlined, and timelines and outcomes identified and agreed upon.

On the other hand, John valued flexibility so, initially, he had no problem adapting his style to meet some of Chris's needs. As a result, John didn't have a problem with a plan being drawn up at the start of the project, and agreed to the suggested steps and timelines. However, he found Chris's need for outcomes to be decided and agreed upon in advance of the work being done frustrating as it was contrary to the more flexible approach of allowing outcomes to emerge.

In honoring his value of flexibility, John also liked to see how things progressed and to then respond accordingly. He started to feel hemmed in by Chris's need to always be kept in the loop and to stick with the plan, no matter what. Over time, the two approaches started to grate and conflict arose from the difference in values. Chris started to see John as undisciplined and wishy-washy while John started to feel constricted and frustrated by Chris's "control-freak" approach to the project.

What was happening was a clash in values—what was important to one was on the other end of the spectrum of what was important to the other. Neither was right, neither was wrong, they were just different. However, the clash was clearly causing a conflict between Chris and John and would continue to do so unless something changed.

From my coaching experience, conflict between two people typically occurs due to values differences. I refer to this conflict as interpersonal conflict.

3. Intra-Team Conflict

While interpersonal conflict is between two people, intra-team conflict refers to conflict occurring specifically within a team. For example, in one intra-team conflict, Paul, the manager, and Mary, the supervisor, were coming into conflict due to Paul's always focusing on the negative while Mary focused on the positive. Tired of the negativity, the team was starting to rally around Mary and Paul was aware that he was becoming very isolated. While this was an interpersonal conflict between two people, due to the levels of the people involved, it was impacting the whole team. As Paul was the manager, nothing was going to change about this conflict until he decided he needed to do something about it.

As it turned out, Paul valued perfection and anything less than that was cause for concern, even if the task didn't require 100 percent. So, if something was 99 percent right, Paul focused on the 1 percent that wasn't perfect, at the expense of acknowledging the 99 percent that was correct. Over time, the rest of the team found this tiring and de-motivating and started looking to Mary, who tended to put more of a positive spin on the team's performance, i.e., she focused on the 99 percent that had been achieved.

As Paul became aware of his value of perfection and the impact it was having on the team, he started to look at ways to adjust his expectations to a more reasonable level. He started to consider each task and determine a reasonable and acceptable working standard, not his platinum standard of 100 percent.

He also started to acknowledge what had gone right and balance that with what was wrong or incomplete. That way, he was better able to maintain perspective and short-circuit his habit of zoning in on the negative. The team noticed his shift and started working with him, instead of against him, and morale in the team started to build again.

Intra-team conflict can be caused by a clash of values between two or more people that spills over into affecting everyone within the team. The more senior the employees involved in the conflict are, the more impacting it becomes on the team as a whole. However, even a conflict between two junior members of staff can impact the rest of the team if they are emotional enough and, over time, the conflict isn't addressed.

Can Personal Values Change?

This example prompts two questions:

— *Do we have to change our values?*
— *Can we change our values?*

In answer to the first question, no, we don't have to change our values. They are ours and each of us can decide to uphold them, modify them, or ignore them, as we see fit. We just live with the consequences of each of those choices.

In answer to the second question, yes, it is possible to change or modify our values, if we so choose. If we recognize repeat patterns that result from the manner in which we define or uphold them and that the negative impact of those patterns outweighs the need to uphold the value(s), a person may decide that the value is no longer of use and decide to alter, completely change, or de-rank it.

In the case of Paul, he still valued perfection but he recognized that his need to uphold it was having increasingly negative results with his team. Rather than either stick with his standard 100 percent or overreact and say, "Okay, let's reduce the standard to 50 percent," he started to appraise each task and select a suitable standard that balanced his own value with what the organization required and what was realistically attainable by the team without de-motivating them. In effect, he modified his value to work more effectively with others.

KEY CONCEPT 4.5

We don't have to change our values but we can, if we so choose to. As we further understand our personal values, they can be modified, their definitions altered, and they can be re-ranked

I have regularly seen individuals who identify a specific value, for example, respect, that they initially define in very narrow terms. As they consider it further and observe the value in practice, they often naturally widen their definition. They still value respect; they just have a more encompassing understanding of it. Since their expectations have expanded, they tend to be less critical of behaviors in others that they previously would have been intolerant of. This results in an effective change in their behavior while they still uphold their value.

Finally, as an individual better understands his or her personal values, the ranking of them, and the possible costs of upholding them, he or she often starts to naturally adjust their ranking.

Take Stephen, who valued honesty and ranked it number one. As he became more aware of his values, he recognized a pattern whereby his driving need to uphold honesty meant that he often delivered messages in a very blunt manner. In his mind, he was upholding his value of honesty but it was causing problems in his relationships with others.

Over time, he recognized that there is a time and place for honesty and that how a message is delivered and the timing of the delivery are hugely important for it to be effective. In effect, he recognized that his value had moved along the spectrum to become a weakness. The adjustment didn't mean that he wasn't upholding his value of honesty; it's just that he realized that he needed to balance his need to be honest with the effectiveness of being honest. He accepted that being honest but destroying relationships wasn't particularly useful to anyone, least of all in the workplace. As a result of this, he bumped honesty down the pecking order. It was still important to him but was no longer his driving value.

4. Inter-Team Conflict

During a values workshop I facilitated with a customer service team, we explored what each of their company's values meant to their members and I then asked them to rank them. As part of the discussion that arose, they highlighted how their team came into a lot of conflict with a particular operations team. So, they decided to take a stab at how they thought the operations team would rank them.

As expected, the rankings were substantially different. The team then considered the behavioral differences that were naturally arising from the ranking differences. While they acknowledged that both teams were upholding company values, they were able to clearly see that the difference in ranking orders was the cause of their conflict. In effect, while meeting the needs of the customer was priority number one for the customer service team, it was bottom of the pile for the operations team, who valued safety. Both teams were upholding company values but the difference in each team's ranking of them was causing conflict.

While the customer service team couldn't change the operations team's perspective, even just understanding the cause of the conflict provided individual team members a huge sense of relief. In addition, since they were better able to see situations from the operations team's point of view, they were better able to present problems and solutions in terms that would influence the other team rather than antagonize them. As a result, they obtained better outcomes for everyone: operations, customer service, and the customer. Instead of focusing on the conflict, team members were able to focus on how to best influence and work with the other team to achieve workable solutions.

Inter-team conflict refers to conflict arising between two (or more) teams due to either different sets of values or differences in ranking company values. For anyone working in a large corporation, this is often referred to as the "silo mentality," e.g., the IT department is separate from the finance department, often culturally as well as functionally, both of which are separate from the operations department, etc. From a design perspective, as a business expands, it often makes sense to group tasks together into a department, from both cost and expertise. Each department is then typically responsible for those functions across the organization as a whole. Therein often lies the problem.

Each department recognizes their responsibility for the functional tasks but not necessarily that they are also explicitly responsible for other aspects, such as customer first, safety, or responsible finance, just some possible company values. Depending on the values, some teams automatically understand how they contribute to upholding a specific value. For example, a customer service team should have a good sense of how they can uphold a value of customer first. Other departments, such as finance or IT, might struggle to connect what they do functionally to such a value and may even uphold a non-company value. This difference in understanding can easily result in conflict arising between the different teams.

The other element to be aware of is, even in an organization that is committed to upholding its values, unless the values have been explicitly ranked, teams might start applying their own rankings and, as we saw above, inter-team conflict can also arise through one team prioritizing one company value while another team prioritizes a different one.

KEY CONCEPT 4.6

Two teams can uphold a company's values and still come into conflict. This conflict can be caused by the two teams implicitly or explicitly ranking the values in different orders. The impact can result in inter-team conflict.

5. Organizational Conflict

Tom valued resourcefulness, which he defined in terms of "not necessarily having the answers, solutions, or resources but being able to find them, as required, so that the job can get done."

An opportunity arose to move to another company. As part of his due diligence, he asked questions about how the new company approached their business. He was assured that achieving results and looking for ways to improve performance were important to the company. This answer reassured Tom that he and the company were sufficiently compatible for it to be a good move for him.

Within weeks, Tom became acutely aware that a great big status quo existed in the new company and that, while achieving results via the current ways was important, when obstacles arose, people just threw up their hands and said it couldn't be done. Every time Tom suggested ways to overcome an obstacle, people would just shrug and say, "Why bother?"

Very quickly, it dawned on Tom that he was a square peg in a round hole. Put another way, he was in conflict with the company's mindset or approach to doing business. Again, it's not that either Tom or the company was right or wrong; it's just that what's important to both of them didn't match.

Returning to Mary and Rick's hotel experience, as the customers, they kept coming into conflict with the hotel and its staff's approach to business. They were advertising the hotel as "family friendly" but Mary and Rick's experience kept highlighting how it was anything but.

Organizational conflict refers to the conflict that arises between an individual and the company, rather than inter-team conflict, which has already been dealt with above. This type of conflict typically arises because the organization says one thing and does another. In relation to values, there are two sources:

— **Source 1:** Company states one set of values (stated values) but actively upholds a different set (actual values)
— **Source 2:** Company states the actual values but behaves inconsistently with them

As we have seen, a company has actual values, whether they actively acknowledge them or not, resulting in everyone sensing "how we do things around here." This is often referred to as the company's culture. Since these values already exist, it becomes a case of identifying what they are, clarifying what they mean, and determining if they are the correct set of values to adhere to going forward. If they are not the right set, then there is a need to identify which ones need to change (comfort values) and what they should ideally change to (missing values).

Not taking the time to understand the actual values and their source and imposing a set that bears little resemblance to the current set causes widespread conflict and cynicism, which we will explore further.

Recap

Actual Values: *A company's set of implicit values that are actually lived, even if they are unspoken. All companies have actual values, whether they are aware of them or not.*

Stated Values: *A set of company values that are selected and explicitly stated, without undertaking the necessary analysis needed to understand what they should be*

Valid Values: *Actual values that have been evaluated as being necessary for the company going forward*

Comfort Values: *Actual values that have been identified as alive but are no longer of use to the company going forward*

Missing Value: *A company value that is identified as necessary for the company's future but is not currently being upheld*

Final Stated Values: *A company's explicitly stated set of values, constructed through careful analysis and with clear awareness of the company's needs. Final stated values are typically a combination of valid and missing values.*

Source 1: Organization States One Set of Values but Upholds Another Set

In this scenario, the company either hasn't taken the time to un-cover the actual values or, for whatever reason, doesn't what to ad-mit what the actual values actually are. Such reasons include: not enough trust to hold the required honest conversations; impatience to define a final set of values; lack of awareness required, both per-sonally and organizationally, to clearly understand the concept of values and their related behaviors; lack of will to undertake the vol-ume of work needed to properly introduce an effective set of values; fear of what will be uncovered; it's just plain hard; or that old chest-nut: not enough time.

For example, while strictly speaking values are neither right or wrong, a company might sense that admitting to a particular value, such as "commercialism at any cost" or "bureaucracy," is not a good thing. So, they hide it and instead publish what they consider to be a much more impressive-sounding list of values. The reality, of course, is that if a company really does value bureaucracy or com-mercialism at any cost, they will behave in ways consistent with it and, as a result, both customers and employees sense it anyway.

Enron is a good example of this. They stated integrity as a value but failed, rather dramatically, to live up to it. At the executive level, there was a sufficient number of individuals who behaved in ways that indicated they valued something else, let's call it "results at any cost," to the point that they engaged in a web of creative accounting and deceit—to the market, the shareholders, the employees, and the customers.

By the time this disparity became self-evident, the resultant conflict was huge. The employees were furious—many of them had lost not only their jobs, but substantial portions of their nest eggs, having invested their savings in Enron shares—and so were the other shareholders. Arthur Anderson's employees were most likely also very upset when it became obvious that they, too, were going to be adversely impacted by their own company being split in two plus the accompanying reputational damage.

Whether the executives involved intended to or not, their ac-tions meant that, along with everyone else, the employees were lied to. They were told integrity was important but here was irrefutable evidence that the organization, as embodied by several key members of the executive team, had no more interest in integrity. Instead, they spent years overstating asset values and understating liabilities to boost the balance sheet, i.e., behaviors more consistent with a value of "results at any cost."

Enron is, of course, an extreme example. Many companies don't go so spectacularly bust but many do engage in the process of stating one set of company values while actively (although perhaps not consciously aware of it) upholding another set. The impact of this is that people sense a mismatch between what is being said by the organization (words) and what is being done (actions). At its most benign, it causes a low-level source of unease that employees often sense but can't quite put their finger on. It is slightly distracting and, at times, might cause an issue, but no show-stoppers.

At its worst, trust breaks down and emotions are widespread, leading to lack of focus on what is really important, i.e., the company's purpose (mission statement). Organizational lack of trust is a very serious matter. An absence of trust within a business just makes everything harder. Leadership, influence, inspiration, and working as a team to achieve agreed-upon goals all become very difficult in a climate of "no trust." Every concession has to be fought long and hard for; staff has to be persuaded, and having to persuade employees, one person at a time, is exhausting and time-consuming. All of this means that the company can't focus on the important things, such as customers, objectives, or growth. Nor can it spot and take advantage of beneficial opportunities because, in the time it would take to persuade people it was a good prospect, the opportunity would be gone.

The longer the mismatch continues, the more wary employees become, the less credible senior management appears, and the breakdown of trust continues on its negative spiral. So, just stating an impressive-sounding set of company values with no effort put into understanding what they mean or how they should be applied to daily business causes unnecessary organizational conflict.

Source 2: Organization States Actual Values but Behaves Inconsistently

The other way a business can generate organizational conflict is by identifying their actual values as their final stated values, which it generally supports, but, for whatever reason, has behaved inconsistently with. This is actually a lot harder to detect as it can arise in a couple of different ways:

1. Sections of the organization uphold the company values regularly but occasionally lapse.
2. One or two executives or senior managers don't buy into the organization's company values and act inconsistently with them.

1. Occasional Lapse in Upholding Values

Occasionally, an employee or a team might behave in ways inconsistent with the company values. It may be they didn't appreciate the way in which their behavior could be interpreted as not upholding the values. Preventing and managing this comes down to how dedicated the company is to communicating the values, upholding them, and following through on consequences for those who don't uphold them. Once it is dealt with fairly quickly and not allowed to get out of hand, the impact of such lapses should be minimal.

2. Individual Executive Not Upholding Values

If an executive or specific team regularly appears to act inconsistently with the rest of the organization, this should be challenged and understood. For example, one company had a core value of added client value. They upgraded their IT systems and provided the necessary training to ensure that all employees were able to adequately support the clients.

However, several of the client service teams failed to see the need to learn the new systems. They didn't feel they needed to know how to use them in order to add value to their clients. They felt that if a client had a query, they could go to the relevant operations team, get the answer, and then revert to the client. They really didn't see that, rather than adding value, this process actually hampered their clients.

In effect, the senior managers in client services just didn't connect their teams' learning the new system with adding value to their clients. Whatever the reasons, the impact was that those teams were behaving inconsistently with the company's values and, by and large, remained unchallenged. This caused conflict between them and the operations teams and, ultimately, with the clients. In the end, some clients actually refused to deal with their client service representative and requested that they work directly with the operations teams.

Letting this fester caused a lot of conflict between the client services and operations teams. It distracted the operations teams from their own work, as they were regularly interrupted to answer random queries. They felt the client service teams should have the ability to answer such questions themselves since their purpose was to liaise with the client. The client service teams didn't see what the big deal was so didn't understand why the operations teams were so hostile towards them.

Once spotted, such a situation should be addressed—not to haul someone over the coals but because not dealing with it leads to further problems down the line. It also implies that not upholding the values is acceptable. If a business is dedicated to realizing the benefits that come with consistently upholding company values, failure to uphold them is not an option.

Strategies to Reduce Sources of Conflict

As we have seen, there are many benefits to be gained by minimizing conflict within the workplace, such as consistent decision-making, positive relationships, increased ability to influence, trust, consistent customer experience, and better employee, team, and organizational performance. Now that we understand the five sources of conflict, how can an organization effectively minimize them?

— **Strategy One:** Personal values program
— **Strategy Two:** Identifying and defining company values

— **Strategy Three:** Understanding values and ranking
— **Strategy Four:** Challenging anti-values behavior

Strategy One: Personal Values Program

Some employees are prone to experiencing conflict more than others while senior managers' personal values have a stronger influence than others' within the workplace. In effect, connecting these two groups of employees with their own values goes a long way to reducing conflict within the company.

A key employee who finds themselves regularly frustrated with others (interpersonal or intra-team conflict) and has poor self-management skills is unlikely to be aware that the cause of their conflict is due to some sort of a clash in values. In addition, such people often experience internal conflict (intrapersonal conflict). Enabling them to access their personal values and understand the source of their conflict can greatly reduce it and minimize the cost to the business.

As the executive team is so influential in defining and implementing a company's culture and approach to business, it is really important that each member is acutely aware of their own personal values, how they rank them, how they connect them through to the company values, and also how they might come into conflict with the company's values. In addition, if they know how their values potentially conflict with those of other executive team members, all the better.

Providing such a development program to the executive team can reduce a source of individual members' intra- and interpersonal conflict. It also lessens organizational conflict, as each executive is more likely to actively support the company values and those that are out of tune will most likely leave. Due to each executive being aligned with the company values, there is also less likelihood of inter-team conflict arising due to a specific team developing a microcosm of alternative values.

The personal values program strategy is based on the idea of ensuring that key employees are aware of what values are, what their personal values are, and how they connect with the company's values. As can be seen in Practical Guide 4.1, the approach should incorporate elements such as ranking personal values, cross-referencing them to the company values, and highlighting any potential sources of conflict between the employee and the company.

Practical Guide 4.1

PERSONAL VALUES PROGRAM

Step 1: Determine the criteria that will decide who will attend the personal values development program.

Step 2: Engage experienced professionals to deliver the program.

Step 3: Determine each participant's personal values, including: definitions; behavioral indicators; ranking of them; cross-reference to company values; identification of any potential conflicts with company values; suitable strategies to overcome those conflicts.

Step 4: In a case where a person's values raise too many conflicts with the organization's, hold a conversation about the level of comfort they feel within the company.

Which employees should attend such a program is up to each company to call but, at a minimum, it should be rolled out to all executives, be that three or twenty.

Some points to consider when making such a decision are:

— *How many grades there are at management level, e.g., in a small business, there might just be the business owner and one or two managers and maybe a supervisor; in a large organization, there might be directors, senior managers, managers, assistant managers, supervisors, etc.*

— *At what grade would an interpersonal conflict become sufficiently negative to become a wider company issue?*

— *Are there specific employees whose performance is hampered by their constantly being engaged in conflict with others?*

— *If new company values have been introduced ,requiring behavioral change, realistically how many grades down need to be included to support such changes?*

— *At what grade do the company's talent management and succession planning programs kick in?*

Broadly speaking, junior employees don't need to be explicitly aware of their own personal values. However, as we will see when we look at ways to embed values into everyday processes, the organization does need to ensure that it is recruiting people whose values complement the company's.

In smaller companies, the program might just be rolled out to the top management team. In larger businesses, a conflict between managers will most likely cause widespread damage, so they should most likely be included in this process. Depending on their role and span of control, first-line managers, e.g., supervisor and team leader level, may or may not need to be included.

For program participants who have a value that obviously clashes with the company's values, time should be spent developing a practical strategy to minimize the likelihood of such clashes.

In a case where an employee's values are clearly out of step, it is important to allow time to explore how comfortable they actually feel working within the business. An employee in such a situation might already feel a sense of relief at finally understanding why they feel like a square peg in a round hole. The awareness might have already prompted them to recognize their own need to move on and find a company that better fits their ethos. During such a conversation, it is very important to stress that neither the individual nor the company is right or wrong. It is just that their expectations and approaches are sufficiently different as to be uncomfortable for both parties.

To successfully implement a personal values program, it is important that employees work with suitably experienced and qualified people, e.g., executive coaches or organizational psychologists. Such professionals should be experienced in working with participants at each phase of the program and, should the need arise, be able to hold such delicate conversations while still maintaining effective relationships.

Strategy Two: Identifying and Defining Company Values

As we have seen, a company that states values without taking the time to understand what the business truly values sets the organization up for conflict. This becomes even more exacerbated if the business engages executive coaches for its employees, as many companies do. By becoming aware of personal values and how they work, these employees are more likely to spot the mismatch. If such an employee is vocal and influential, he or she may start verbalizing the mismatch, causing more people to recognize it, resulting in a rapidly escalating problem.

Strategy two focuses on a company taking the time to honestly create a set of final stated values by capturing and analyzing the actual values, ditching any comfort values, and incorporating any relevant missing values, as outlined in Practical Guide 4.2. Creating a set of values that can be clearly communicated and will be actively supported reduces the likelihood of conflict arising through misunderstandings and inconsistencies.

Practical Guide 4.2

INDENTIFYING AND DEFINING FINAL STATED COMPANY VALUES

Step 1: Recognize and acknowledge the existing organizational conflict that exists.

Step 2: Determine if there is an honest interest or will to do something about it.

Step 3: If there is the will, then honestly identify the company's actual values and each of the executive team members' personal values.

Step 4: Assess whether the actual values are of use to how the company wants to achieve its purpose. Split them into valid values and comfort values. Identify and define any missing values.

Step 5: Roll out the final stated values and monitor change.

Step 1:
If a set of values is stated but not understood very well, it can be difficult to recognize that they are not being upheld. An awareness of what values are, what the company's values are, and how those values would most likely translate into behaviors, as well as having the insight into the messages that are actually being sent out, is needed to be able to recognize and acknowledge what is happening.

Step 2:
Honestly determine if the will or interest in doing something about the current level of conflict exists, since just imposing a new set of values isn't going to change the situation. If the will isn't there, the reality is that the situation will continue until either (a) it becomes such a crisis that it can no longer be ignored and something has to be done; or (b) turnover at the executive/senior management team levels is sufficiently high and their replacements hold personal values more in line with the stated values, so that the culture will change naturally.

Not to point out the obvious, but the "head in the sand" approach will take years to sufficiently resolve itself, causing untold damage in the meantime and the ongoing cost of organizational underperformance. Waiting for a crisis to reach rock bottom before dealing with it tends to require a lot more effort to get out of the hole and is much more costly, in terms of time, money, and energy.

Step 3:
If the will to do something about it exists, the next step is to spend time honestly identifying both the company's actual values and each executive team member's personal values (see Practical Guide 4.1 for suggested approach). A comparison between the stated and actual values can be undertaken and the level of overlap will become apparent. Through identifying each executive's personal values, insight into the sources of the actual values can also be identified.

Step 4:
Determine whether the actual values are valid for how the company wants to achieve its purpose. Those values that are considered of no benefit are the organization's comfort values and need to be phased out. Those values that are still valid become part of the final stated values. If there are obvious gaps, missing values that will realistically be supported, given the executive team's mix of personal values, should be identified. The meaning of the company's set of final stated values should be defined and accompanied by

examples of what they look like in everyday terms. It might also be beneficial to define the comfort values and their related behaviors so that employees can recognize when they slip back into their comfort zone.

Step 5:
Roll out the company's set of final values and monitor its impact. That sentence is easier written than done, of course. This step takes a huge amount of commitment from the executive team and a vigilance to ensure they are being upheld, which we will look at in more detail in the next chapter. For now, it is important to understand that a company can unwittingly cause organizational conflict and such conflict can be costly to the business.

Strategy Three: Understanding Values and Ranking
When introducing values within an organization, be they personal, team, or company values, it's important to also introduce and explore the concept of ranking them. As we have seen, one team might rank a set of values differently than another, causing inter-team conflict to arise. Or different employees might rank the company values differently, potentially causing interpersonal or intra-team conflict.

Strategy three looks at exploring the ranking of values at two levels within the organization:

— *Personal values*
— *Company values*

Level One: Ranking of Personal Values
If everyone has their own personal values, is anyone's values more important than anyone else's? As humans, it's very easy for each of us to gravitate toward concluding that our values are more important than everyone else's. The only problem is that many other employees also think that way. As outlined in Key Concept 4.7, no one set of values is "better than" or "worse than" any other set of values.

KEY CONCEPT 4.7

One value or set of values is not "better than" or "worse than" another value or set of values; they are just different

In the case of interpersonal conflict, by each party understanding and accepting this key concept, perceptions of the conflict change. It is easier to de-personalize the conflict and accept that the situation has arisen through values differences, not because one person is trying to "get at" the other. So, the ranking of personal values strategy focuses on explaining that one set of values can't be ranked as more or less important than another set; they are equal but different. Such understanding should reduce interpersonal conflict.

Level Two: Ranking Company Values

The second part of this strategy focuses on the company taking the time to rank its values, providing guidance to all employees as to the order in which the values are important. Not clearly ranking company values allows ambiguity to creep in and for teams to rank them differently, creating an environment for interpersonal, intra- or inter-team, and organizational conflict to surface.

Strategy Four: Challenging Anti-Values Behavior

The above strategies clearly require a considerable commitment to both the idea of company values and to incorporating them into the business. The final strategy focuses on preventing that good work from being undone by ensuring employees understand, connect with, and remain aligned to the values through challenging behaviors, actions, and decisions that don't appear to support them.

Use of the word "challenge" here is not meant in the sense of "accuse." A behavior or decision can be challenged by asking non-personal questions such as, "How does that behavior uphold the values?" or "What was the ultimate driver in coming to that decision?" In effect, "challenge" is being used in the sense of raising the topic and holding the conversation in order to explore perceptions and interpretations, and to learn from the incident.

Practical Guide 4.3 provides a suggested approach that can be drawn on when having a values conversation. During the conversation, it would be worthwhile exploring with the individual what their personal values are and how they might be conflicting with the organization's value of X (e.g., efficiency, adding value, etc.). Such focus sheds light on the conflict while allowing the conversation to stay neutral. If there is a natural conflict of values, then it's important to stress what the company's values are and that ultimately these need to be upheld by everyone, including this employee.

Should this get a negative reaction, the next step could be to explore what would happen if everyone insisted on upholding their own values. It would lead to chaos.

If this isn't yielding an acceptable outcome, the next step might be to allow the employee time to reflect on what values are, that different organizations have other sets of values (none of which are right or wrong, just different), and that all employees have a choice and should spend time selecting the company that best reflects their own values. This should help the individual further understand the role of values within the business and the importance of their being upheld by everyone.

Prior to engaging in such a conversation, it is important to consider that the individual might well have their own perspective on the values and what they perceive as inconsistencies in honoring them within the company. Should such insights be shared, they should be explored and considered further to determine if there is truth in them.

If the behavior doesn't change after such a conversation, and it hasn't already been included as a performance objective, a behavioral objective outlining what is required can be added in their next appraisal. In the event that the objective isn't achieved, it should be addressed as per the company's regular performance management process.

VALUES CONVERSATION

Step 1: Recognize that an individual's behaviors and actions are not upholding a company value. Have specific examples at hand.

Step 2: During conversation, raise the company value that is of concern and explore their understanding of what it means in everyday life, particularly in their area.

Step 3: Discuss their personal values, compare them to the company's values, and explore if they have an issue with upholding the specific value of concern.

Step 4: Explain the importance of the company's values, how everyone needs to support them, and ask how they can actively uphold them.

Step 5: If they react negatively, explore what would happen if everyone upheld their own values at the expense of the company's.

Step 6: If a resolution is still not satisfactory, incorporate it into performance management as a behavioral objective and review as part of that process, if this has not already been done. If it has and the objective has clearly not been met, then proceed as per performance management process.

Challenging unsupportive behaviors and decisions sends out a very clear message that the company values are important and need to be supported at all times. A requirement here is that such a process must be upheld by all levels within the organization, particularly by the executive team. If values conversations were being held with middle managers while executives blatantly flaunted the values, organizational conflict would be rife and such conversations could get very heated.

The four strategies suggest some ways that conflict throughout the company can be reduced. Some strategies can be brought in piecemeal, e.g., a personal values program could be introduced within a team or a department, while others clearly need to be introduced at the organizational level, such as identifying and defining company values. Successfully introducing and implementing all four strategies together should go a long way toward reducing the sources of conflict, and freeing employees up to focus on the company's mission statement and supporting the company's values.

Chapter Four Summary

— *Conflict arises through differing sets of expectations, be they expectations arising from values or desires.*

— *Conflict is costly for an organization. Such costs include: poor decision-making; deterioration of relationships; mistrust; hording information and lack of co-operation; loss of focus on goals, resulting in underperformance; sick and stress leave; turnover and loss of knowledge and skills.*

— *Minimizing conflict results in organizational benefits such as: clear, effective, and consistent decisions; effective relationships; sharing of information and co-operation; better influencing ability; focus on achieving goals and overall increase in performance.*

— *There are five levels of conflict:*

   ○ *Intrapersonal—conflict within an employee*
   ○ *Interpersonal—conflict between two employees*
   ○ *Intra-team—conflict within a team*
   ○ *Inter-team—conflict between two or more teams*
   ○ *Organizational—conflict between an employee or customer and the organization*

— *To reduce and minimize conflict, four suggested strategies are:*

   ○ *Strategy one: Personal values program*
   ○ *Strategy two: Identifying and defining company values*
   ○ *Strategy three: Understanding values and ranking*
   ○ *Strategy four: Challenging anti-values behavior*

CHAPTER FIVE

Identifying Company Values

If values are so important to an organization, how can a business go about identifying what their company values are?

Some organizations go to huge lengths and effort to find meaningful values. For example, in 2003, IBM[10] decided that it was time to revisit and update their core values, something that hadn't been done since its founding in 1911. Leveraging off their proprietary technology, they invited fifty thousand staff to engage in an online discussion over a three-day period. From this, their final stated values became:

— *Dedication to every client's success*
— *Innovation that matters—for our company and for the world*
— *Trust and personal responsibility in all relationships*

As Samuel J. Palmisano openly admits, some of the comments were very painful to read, such as the company was crippled by bureaucracy (could be considered an actual value); he was also open

---

10   *Harvard Business Review* Interview, December 2004, "Leading Change When Business is Good, An interview with Samuel J. Palmisano by Paul Hemp and Thomas A. Steward"

and committed enough to not shut the experience down, a key element to the success of the project. The strength of this action should not be underestimated as many an executive would not have been nearly so courageous.

Even for someone not aware of the process IBM underwent to agree on their values, upon reading them, one can see that they immediately stand out from many other "typical" company values as being considered and thoughtful. They are also quite embracing. Looking at "trust and personal responsibility"; this is extended to "all relationships." It's not reserved for just clients or staff. Similarly, their definition of innovation is very inspiring—while they want IBM to do well, they also want to make a difference in how the world works.

Invoking a fifty-thousand-way conversation via technology is one end of the spectrum available to identifying company values. Let's look at the other end of the spectrum, which, I suspect, is the more regularly used end. The following are two of my favorite stories of how companies have actually approached identifying their values.

The first story is from a company I was invited to visit. On the appointed day, I met with the CEO and another member of the management team. The CEO explained that their problem was that, year in, year out, the management team set goals in January but, by year end, they found they had failed to achieve them. As CEO, he recognized this repeat pattern and wanted to change it. Hence the reason I was there.

Prior to our meeting, the CEO mentioned that he was a huge fan of Robin Sharma and *The Monk Who Sold His Ferrari*. Excited about the opportunity of working with such an enlightened executive, I started reading the book in advance of our appointment.

During the meeting, as part of assessing where they were at, I inquired if they had company values, which were duly brought up on the screen. I asked where these had come from, to be told that the CEO had introduced them. My next question was whether the values had been discussed with the management team. The response was, "No, but all the team had been given the book to read."

It would be fair to say that the CEO and I didn't really click. Despite the fact that he had stated values such as humility, patience, and honesty, he was in such a huge hurry to get to where he wanted to go that he wanted answers and solutions now and was not open to taking the time to consider where the source of the blockage within the company was coming from. While he had stepped out of the room for a minute, I asked the other manager what she thought the lack of achievement was due to. The answer came back through her description of how the CEO would regularly sweep in and redirect what was to be done, at the expense of the original goals. However, he couldn't see that his behavior was both the cause of the repeat pattern and in conflict with his stated values of patience and honesty, and none of the senior managers were about to tell him.

Recognizing that we weren't going to achieve anything by working together, we parted company but I finished the book anyway. To my great amusement, but not surprise, I came to the page where the monk espouses the values of, you guessed it, humility, patience, and honesty, along with industry, compassion, and courage, the other values the CEO had shared with me.

Now, don't get me wrong; these are all very valid and appropriate values to have *for someone who truly espouses them.* The problem for this CEO was that he didn't actually personally value many of them. During the course of our one meeting alone, he displayed a distinct lack of humility and patience, alongside a complete lack of honesty, with himself and the rest of the management team.

The reality was that until the CEO dealt with his impulsive behavior, the management team was never going to achieve their annual targets or break the pattern, much to everyone's continued frustration. Selecting the company's values out of a book, without any consideration as to how valid or appropriate they are to the company and its purpose, is definitely one way to go. As we can see, though, it's not a particularly effective approach, unless those values happen to genuinely coincide with the company's actual values.

The second story came from a marketing director of an international advertising agency. The marketing director herself had undergone some difficult times with the CEO and had been recounting them to me. Out of curiosity, I inquired if they had company values. The response was: yes, they did, but values were of no use in their organization. Intrigued by such a response from somebody so senior and in marketing, I asked how they had been selected.

She went on to tell me how she had been tasked by the CEO to come up with a list of company values. She duly did this and presented them back to the executive team, who went on to completely ignore them. Highly amused, I asked if they had spent any time discussing the meaning of the selected values or how they were to be used within the business. I could see the slow dawning of comprehension spread across her face: "Ah, perhaps that's where we went wrong."

While a company's values can and should be used in marketing material, actually tasking the marketing director to come up with them on his or her own is probably not the most effective way of selecting meaningful values. If nothing else, unless the marketing director is actually working in a dedicated marketing business, marketing tends to be a support function and not involved in the actual daily delivery of what the company does.

Secondly, marketing's take on values is somewhat different to that of an organizational design specialist or executive coach. While a company's values support the brand, they are not the same as an actual brand.

Comparing the two stories, both have a few things in common that we can learn from:

- *Both selected a list of "words" and thought this was enough.*
- *Neither took the time to discuss the values, their meanings, associated behaviors, or how the values should be used within the company with the rest of the executive team.*
- *Neither spent time defining the words or exploring the types of actions and behaviors that might uphold those words.*
- *Neither really understood how values should be used in everyday life and, by extension, nor did anyone else in either company.*
- *Neither of them spent any time rolling the values out to the rest of the company or communicating them.*

KEY CONCEPT 5.1

Tips To Successfully Leverage Company Values

— *Naming values is just the start of creating company values.*

— *Values need to include definitions and behavioral indicators.*

— *The executive team needs to understand how they are going to uphold and support the values.*

— *Time should be taken to roll the values out across the organization.*

— *There should be widespread understanding of how the values are to be applied to everyday business life.*

— *Behaviors and actions that don't uphold the values should be challenged.*

If a company genuinely wants to identify and incorporate a set of final stated values into their everyday lives, then there are some very valid lessons, of the "what not to do" type, to be taken from these observations.

Whose Values Matter Most?

As we saw earlier, everyone has personal values and one set isn't better or worse than another; they're just different. So, when a group of people is gathered together, such as in a company, many values are in play. Some people's values will dovetail with others while some will naturally clash.

From the organization's perspective, it can't have numerous sets of values in play at the same time. It needs one clear set of values that all employees are expected to uphold. So, organizationally, the question is:

Whose personal values matter most?

To answer this question, let's take a quick look at how companies work. Employees work in companies in exchange for money to pay for their basic needs (e.g., rent/mortgage, food, clothes, utilities, etc.) and some of their wants (e.g., car, holidays, nicer/more clothes, etc.).

Once these needs are met, they move into the area of wanting to belong or connect with the organization. For most people, this translates to "can I tolerate the people I work with, do I like the people I work with, can I deal with the way things are done around here?" One element of "belonging" is feeling connected to how the company approaches doing business, often referred to as the "culture."

If they feel that connection, i.e., they are working in a company that is palatable enough for them (let's face it, most people settle for a reasonable fit), many (not all) will start to want to move up the ranks or gain wider experience. They start wanting the titles, the authority, the power, the responsibility, and the opportunities to meet their needs of status and esteem.

Keeping in mind that we can attain a certain level of status and then, due to circumstances, drop down a level or two (e.g., we could be fired, demoted, or made redundant), most people want to keep their heads down and hold on to what they have. So, they learn to look up the line and see what is expected of them.

This expectation isn't centered just around results but also what is expected of them behaviorally. They look to see "how" the boss wants people to behave. Since the boss often doesn't explicitly say "how" s/he wants people to behave, people make two assumptions, often unconsciously. One, they assume that the boss wants them to behave in the same way the boss behaves. Two, they look to see what behaviors get rewarded and assume these represent the desired approach.

So, people at the lower levels behave the way they see their line manager behave or replicate the actions they saw the line manager exhibit and get promoted (rewarded) for. In turn, the line managers mimic the next level(s) up and this continues right up to the CEO.

Getting back to the question of "whose values matter most," the obvious answer is that the CEO and executive team's values matter most. Ultimately, it is this group of people's personal values, behaviors, and actions that are most widely replicated. This is also the team that typically identifies and signs off on the company values in the first place.

KEY CONCEPT 5.2

While every employee has their own personal values, organizationally, the CEO and executive team's personal values matter most as they have the widest influence on upholding the company's values.

What does this mean for a company looking to identify and implement a set of final stated values?

First and foremost, it means the executive team *MUST* understand and buy into the values. If they don't, the company is wasting its time and resources, as we saw illustrated with both the book and the marketing director stories. Not only that, but introducing a set of company values without this buy-in will most likely introduce needless sources of conflict and its related impact on performance, as we already saw in the chapter on conflict.

Returning to IBM, the democratic manner in which they chose to identify their values carried a huge risk in that the executive team could have ended up in a position of having to uphold a set of values that they didn't personally connect with. If this had happened, and they weren't consistently able to live up to the final stated values, the fallout would have been enormous. It would have resulted in employees witnessing disconnect between the final stated values they had agreed on and the executive team's actions, resulting in their questioning the whole point of the exercise. The resultant conflict would have been huge as cynicism, mistrust, and misdirected energy railroaded employee performance. As IBM's executive team was committed to the process and the outcomes, this didn't happen.

To successfully incorporate values into a culture in any meaningful way, it is vitally important for the executive team to actively understand and/or undertake the following:

1. What company values are and are not
2. The difference between "stated" values and "actual" values
3. What their own personal values are
4. What the company's actual values are
5. Evaluating the company's actual values
6. Defining final stated values
7. Ranking final stated values
8. Ways the executive team need to uphold final stated values
9. How to communicate values throughout the company
10. How to incorporate values into daily business

Since points one to seven deal with identifying and signing off on a company's set of final stated values while points eight to ten deal with how to effectively roll them out across the company, this chapter will explore points one to seven while the next chapter will explore points eight to ten.

Recap

Personal Values: Personal values are an internal set of standards that each of us expects ourselves, and others, to live up to. These standards are sufficiently worthwhile that we spend extra time and effort behaving in ways that uphold them.

Company Values: Company values represent the company's internal set of standards it expects everyone within the organization, including the executive team, to live up to. They embody the business's approach to achieving its purpose.

1. What Company Values Are and Are Not

We all have personal values, even the executive team. Similarly, all companies have a collective set of values that they uphold. Both sets of values exist whether the individual or company is explicitly aware of them or not. Since a company's values are generated through collective influence, the executive team members' personal values are most influential on the actual values.

Company values can be thought of as a set of ideals, an ethos, or a philosophy as to how the organization approaches the business of doing business. They are generally incorporated as part of the mission statement, which is an articulation of the vision. Company values are distinct from competency frameworks[11], even though both may have behavioral indicators.

Values tend to be less specific than competencies and work at a higher level. For example, values are often incorporated into a company's mission statement while a competency framework is more likely to be incorporated into processes such as recruitment, performance management, and talent development. However, best practice would recommend that they support each other.

For example, a company value such as respect might well be underpinned by behavioral indicators denoted in competencies such as communication, teamwork, and interpersonal relationships. In this case, some of the actions that demonstrate respect are very likely to also be incorporated into these competencies' behavioral indicators.

Possible communication indicators might include: listens to other people's points of view; considers other people's point of view; asks questions to find out what other people think. These are all good examples of behaviors that also support a value of respect.

Behavioral indicators for teamwork might include: actively keeps the team in the loop; seeks ways to help teammates to achieve results; when time allows, consults with the team. Again, these actions might be considered ways to uphold respect.

Lastly, behavioral indicators for interpersonal relationships might include: builds two-way relationships; develops strong

---

11 More information on what a competency framework is can be found in appendix B.

empathy to enable other points of view to be considered; adapts communication style to match others'. Likewise, these could all be ways to uphold respect.

As we can see in Diagram 5.1: Hierarchy of Vision, Mission Statement, Values, and Competency Framework, values sit as part of the mission statement, which sits above the competency framework, which, in turn, underpins objectives, recruitment, and talent management. The closer the alignment between the company's understanding of their values and the behavioral indicators of their competency framework, the more effective both will be.

Diagram 5.1: Hierarchy of Vision, Mission Statement, Values, and Competency Framework

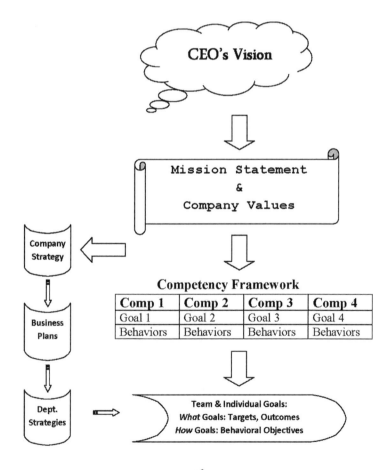

2. Difference between Stated and Actual Values

As we saw in some of the stories above, selecting some "important-sounding" words, from a book or elsewhere, that bear no relation to the company's approach to business, or to the executive team's personal values, isn't going to magically turn them into living company values.

For any given company, excluding start-ups, actual values have already evolved and are in-situ, whether the executive team is consciously aware of them or not. Not only that, but the executive team is already supporting them.

So if a company already has actual values that have evolved, why bother spending time trying to identify them? The issue is that these actual values are usually not explicitly named or understood. They often clash with each other, they are not consistently upheld, they are often at odds with what the company says, and they can cause a lot of confusion and conflict.

In addition, from the organization's perspective, some of the actual values might not be particularly desirable. For example, should several of the executive team members value avoiding conflict, there is a good chance that this value has evolved into an actual value and is causing all sorts of problems, such as ignoring performance issues or not tackling a bully, that the executives don't want to admit to.

Painful as it might be, if such a value is part of a company's actual values, acknowledging it and the damage it is causing is very important and necessary, if there is any hope of genuine change.

Can stated and actual values be the same, i.e., can a company state a set of values that happens to exactly match the implicit values they already uphold? It is possible that the two lists could match, but unlikely. Many companies have one or two actual values that, in an ideal world, they wouldn't choose. Since a set of stated values is typically a wish list, it is unlikely that there would be a perfect match with the actual values.

To summarize, actual values are those values that are currently in-situ, regardless of whether the company is consciously aware of them or not. Stated values are those that are up on the wall plaque and quoted as part of the mission statement, without having undertaken the necessary due diligence. It is possible that a company's stated values match their actual values but usually they don't.

3. Understanding the Executive Team's Personal Values

In one very interesting project, a small professional services company was undergoing a rebranding exercise and the CEO was conscious of not making a marketing promise to the world if his company wasn't going to be able to deliver on it. In short, he wanted to ensure that his company "walked the talk."

As part of the project, we identified the need to define a set of final stated company values and cross-reference them to the branding message, to confirm that, if they upheld the revised values, they would naturally deliver on the brand.

I spent some time with the CEO, understanding what his personal values were, what added value he saw his company delivering to clients, what he wanted to achieve with the business, and what gaps he had already identified. In addition, I met with the other two members of the executive team and worked with each of them to identify their personal values and what they saw were the needs of the organization, etc.

I then analyzed the data, looking for the similarities and the outliers, cross-referencing the findings to the business's needs, and, finally, I identified five values, with definitions, that I presented back to the executive team for discussion.

As each of them was now aware of what values were and of their own personal values, they were able to relate to both the suggested values and their definitions. Among themselves, they discussed, finalized, and signed off on their set of final stated values, and threw out their old set. As it turned out, the final set of values was made up of actual values that were not being consistently supported by all three executives.

As mentioned, there was a branding element to the project and, as part of that, the branding consultant interviewed several of the company's clients and fed those insights into the mix. The final stated values were then cross-referenced back to the collective client feedback. What became obvious was that what the clients valued most from this service provider was very much in keeping with the types of behavior that the business would naturally deliver if they consistently upheld their actual values.

Unconsciously, the business was attracting clients that connected with the executive team's actual values rather than the type of clients they theoretically should have been attracting from their stated values. This project reinforced the connection between a company's actual values and the executive team's personal values.

As we saw during the chapter on conflict, having stated values that bear no resemblance to actual values causes more hassle than it's worth and undermines the performance of the company. We have also seen that the executive team's personal values are hugely influential in shaping and upholding company values. So, if their personal values are not understood or acknowledged, there is little likelihood of successfully introducing a set of final stated values that will be supported.

I learned this insight the really hard, frustrating way. It was my very first time working on a company values project. As part of a wider remit, the executive team agreed to introduce company values in support of other pieces of organizational design (OD) work that were being undertaken.

The company values process[12] used allowed the group to identify the current actual values (valid and comfort values), the missing values, and the required final stated values (valid plus missing values), along with definitions of each value. In effect, they had identified the actual values, undertaken a values gap analysis, highlighted missing values, and agreed on a set of defined final stated values.

The final part of the workshop even focused on identifying practical steps that the team could take to shift the missing values into becoming living final stated values. It should have been a roaring success, right? It wasn't. Where did it go wrong?

Unfortunately for everyone, the CEO had other plans. She had moved into the role while the other pieces of OD work were being completed, and, in retrospect, probably only agreed to continue with the values workshop because she felt she couldn't say no at that point.

---

12 For a detailed description of the approach taken, see appendix C.

Upon mature reflection, what I hadn't done was take the time to assess what each executive's personal values were. Looking back, when it came to finalizing the values, there was definitely tension among the group as to which values should and shouldn't be included.

Numbers won the day but they lost the war. Perhaps some of the final values didn't sit well with the CEO's personal values but, since we hadn't done that piece of work, the conflict was never brought to light. Instead, as CEO, she pulled the plug on the whole project and I was told in no uncertain terms that she wasn't going to present a list of values to the company that she felt was not going to be supported.

That set of company values never even made it as far as the wall plaque, let alone the website. Instead, it languished in her desk drawer for the remainder of her tenure.

While I felt decidedly frustrated at her lack of support, not to mention the cost of the wasted exercise, as I look back now, she was absolutely right in her decision because the reality was there were several executives, including herself, who were never going to support the final values—in this case not because we had just plucked some nice-sounding words from the air, but because the values we had actually selected didn't fully underpin those of several key members of the executive team and, in particular, the CEO's.

This story effectively highlights the importance of being aware of each executive team member's own personal values. Had we spent the time uncovering them and ensuring that some of the more common ones were supported, particularly some of the CEO's, she might well have felt more in-tune with the final list and given it her full support.

One obvious question that arises from this is:

> *Does this mean that each of every executive member's values must be included?*

The answer is no. It is not possible, nor would it be desirable, to incorporate everyone's personal values into the company's values. The organization is a separate entity to each individual executive, albeit it is heavily influenced by them as a whole.

For most executives, they are likely to have one or two values that they do not share with the wider team, and that's okay. Where it becomes a concern is when an executive's personal values are completely at odds with the rest of the team, i.e., they might have only one or two personal values in common with the wider team. If they are not already feeling it, this executive will most likely start to feel very uncomfortable as it dawns on them that they are at odds with the rest of their peers. If they have already sensed this disconnect but not understood its source, at a minimum they will probably be relieved to finally understand the underlying cause.

As painful as this may be, it is actually really important to uncover such a disparity for two main reasons:

a. Since the executive has personal values, whether aware of them or not, he or she is most likely behaving in ways that uphold them within their business area. This means that within that unit, people are acting in accordance with this executive's personal values, not those of the company. It is very likely that this department, business unit, or function is culturally out of synch with the rest of the organization, i.e., there is a micro-culture within this area, most likely causing inter-team conflict.
b. Such existence of a micro-culture can cause confusion within the team or department, as they are being told one thing by the organization and experiencing something completely different on the ground, resulting in organizational conflict.

Take, for example, a financial services company that valued teamwork. Ron, a senior manager, just didn't see the importance of it and actively behaved in ways more consistent with personal ambition. Within the organization, there was a strong focus on information-sharing, cross-training, collaboration, and sharing success. This typically led to positive engagement and effective results.

Ron really just didn't get any of this so he never bothered with any of it. He regularly took all the glory for his team's successes and, when things went wrong, without thinking, he pointed the finger of blame at others. Ron's team gradually become aware of his approach and started to withdraw their support. They stopped going the extra mile for the team, began engaging in CYA actions, and went to great lengths to subtly let managers and senior managers in other departments know what was going on. They also started to actively look for other opportunities, either internally or externally, to leave Ron to his own devices. Since this was impacting Ron's own performance and therefore thwarting his desires in relation to his value of personal ambition, this caused him to become very aggressive with the team, further worsening the situation.

Ron was completely at odds with the rest of the company, and his staff could see and feel this. They looked at other teams working in harmony, achieving results, being protected by their managers if something went wrong, while they were hung out to dry by Ron. Other senior managers found this behavior unsettling and inappropriate. They winced every time Ron either took all the credit for successes or started to blame others, including his team, for mistakes.

There was a very real cost to the organization, too. It was no longer getting the full benefit of the people in this area because their attention was being diverted away from getting the job done toward finding ways to undermine Ron. Relative to the rest of the organization and the team's capability, the employees were underperforming and staff turnover was high. For those that left the company, it was losing valuable experience and knowledge.

Unfortunately for Ron, he was a square peg in a round hole. He just didn't get that one of the core values of the company was teamwork or that his value of personal ambition was in conflict with it, causing a lot of distress for his team. In addition, his own performance was being hampered, as his team no longer played ball with him.

Examining this situation, it brings up an obvious question:

Does it have to be the case of "teamwork" or "personal ambition"?

The answer is no, it doesn't have to be an either/or situation. It is very viable that a person could uphold teamwork and personal ambition. Again, it comes down to definitions. Given Ron's behavior, it is likely that, if he was being completely honest, his perception, and therefore definition, of personal ambition is defined in terms of his success at the expense of others. Another person's definition of personal ambition might follow "success for one, success for all," to paraphrase the Three Musketeers. Unlike Ron's mindset, this is a more inclusive, win-win approach to personal ambition, which can work in conjunction with another value such as teamwork. This is just one example of how values can work against each other or can support each other by applying one as part of another value.

Depending on how out of synch an executive is with those around them will determine how best to proceed. Having one value out of synch may not be the end of the world. Recognizing the cause of the conflict, accepting it, and devising a strategy to deal with it can minimize the problem. By the executive being made aware of their personal value and the conflict it is causing between them and the organization, he or she may even decide to modify their values or re-rank them.

From the business's perspective, as suggested in Practical Guide 4.3, a conversation may need to be had with the executive and performance measures specifically put in place to ensure alignment with the company's values. Taking this step provides a very clear message that the company's values are important and must be upheld by everyone. It is then up to the executive whether they want to engage or not.

If two or three of an executive's personal values are in conflict with the company's values, this is getting more serious. It might be time for the executive and the CEO to reconsider how well he or she "fits in with" and is aligned with the organization's way of achieving its purpose.

While having a conversation around an executive's personal values can feel uncomfortable for many people, such an exchange is beneficial for both sides. The executive is probably struggling with the culture anyway but doesn't understand the cause. I have found that when people actually understand that their conflict is due to a clash in values, it brings with it a huge sense of relief. The employee can then decide whether they want to continue with this company or find a new employer whose values they are more aligned with, thus reducing their personal turmoil.

The organization also benefits from having such a conversation. In the case of Ron, a serious conversation outlining the impact his approach is having on both the executive team and other employees might well be enough to either change his behavior or prompt him to move on. Sometimes, it's just time to move on. In the event that nothing is done to address the situation, Ron's behavior will continue to undermine the company's values.

In summary, it is important to understand the executive team's personal values and to ensure that the common values are captured in the final stated values. Not all personal values need to be included but a sufficient number should be in order to maximize the ease with which the executive team can support the final stated values. Should it arise that a particular executive's values have little overlap with the final stated values, holding a conversation to determine how comfortable they would be with supporting the company's values is worthwhile.

4. Identifying a Company's Actual Values

This section will look at different options that can be used to identify actual values. Before doing so, it is important to understand why this step is necessary.

Reasons to Identify Actual Values

As we have seen, an organization's actual values are a combination of what the executive team exhibits, what is rewarded, and what is and isn't considered when making decisions. These then ripple throughout the workplace. In some cases, it is also possible that some values are a legacy from departed executives that the current team's values have yet to dislodge.

Understanding the organization's current actual values, rather than just introducing a set of stated values, is important for the following reasons:

— *Just blindly introducing a set of stated values will not make them be effectively implemented.*

— *The opportunity to become aware of the actual values and their sources is lost.*
— *Conflicts may arise between the actual values and the stated values, causing underperformance. Strategies cannot be put in place to minimize the impact of such potential conflicts due to lack of awareness.*
— *Some of the actual values might well continue to be valid and don't need to be changed.*

Declaring a new set of stated values that are inconsistent with the actual values will not change employees' behavior if they don't see any actual evidence that (1) the new values are being modeled from the top, providing concrete evidence that the final set of values are actually important, and (2) the behaviors associated with the old actual values are actively seen as no longer acceptable.

To be able to model the final stated values and to actively dissuade people from behaving in the old way, an awareness of what the actual values are, and what their associated behaviors look like, is required.

For example, take a company that has an actual value of risk aversion. On the ground, this translates into managers not making decisions in case they get it wrong. They do this by postponing decision-making, by asking for more data or another report to be produced, by insisting a business case must be put forward, or they escalate it up to the next level. Basically, they do anything that bats the decision-making into next week, month, or year.

Risk aversion became an actual value in this company because, every time something went wrong, the organization's response was to play the "blame game": what went wrong, who approved this, who made the decision? Whoever made the decision becomes the scapegoat (the "reward"), so managers learned very quickly not to make another decision, if it could be at all avoided. The impact of this was that nobody would sign off on a decision and every decision was escalated to the highest level.

As you can imagine, or may even have experienced, this behavior inevitably frustrates the executive team, who feels that their managers don't take ownership or responsibility. It also slows down the organization's effectiveness in responding to situations or to changes in the market. A natural response might be to introduce a new value of innovation or accountability in an attempt to counteract the behaviors associated with risk aversion. However, by not taking the time to name the actual value or to understand the cause of it, just introducing a new value to counteract the current behavioral pattern is pointless. Managers are just not going to risk embracing "innovation" or "accountability" because they were told to, out of fear of what will happen when it all goes wrong.

By not taking the time to uncover the source of risk aversion, the executive team is unaware that by blaming, they are actually causing the behavior. Nor can they recognize that they need to stop naming and shaming and, instead, start using mistakes as neutral learning opportunities. If they fail to understand the chain reaction, risk aversion will continue on its merry way, much to the frustration of the executive team and an unsuccessful introduction of the new value.

To break this cycle, recognizing the cause has to happen first. From there, a strategy can be created to break the scapegoating habit and the executive team can support each other in changing their own behaviors first. For example, when something does go wrong and one executive starts asking, "Who allowed this to happen?" the others can point out that it's not important "who" allowed it to happen but "how it happened."

Once the executive team starts focusing on "how," i.e., what were the contributory factors that resulted in the mistake, managers will see that they are not being hung out to dry and, over time, will start engaging in the learning, resulting in a building up of their confidence, a further deepening of their abilities, and, most likely, less errors happening in the first place.

It's worth noting that an actual value of risk aversion can often result from a necessary value such as safety. In many industries, safety is a requirement. By default, it must feature in a company's approach to doing business. However, if safety becomes the number-one ranked value, and errors and mistakes are responded to by blaming and scapegoating, the impact is that safety moves along the spectrum toward risk aversion, becoming a weakness.

While it is important to recognize that certain situations will arise whereby values come into conflict and, in such instances, one value does need to outrank others and appropriately so, it is also important to be aware that constantly overusing one value, at the expense of the others, can turn a strength into a weakness. In the example above, safety had morphed into risk aversion, which became damaging to the company's ability to perform or grow. On the whole, values should work in balance, with no one value being constantly applied at the expense of the others. Rankings only need be used when a situation arises that brings two or more values into conflict.

Options to Identify Actual Values

There are many ways to identify a company's actual values. This section outlines some suggested approaches, with advantages and disadvantages to consider. It should be noted that, regardless of the method or combination of methods selected, anonymity should be maintained as much as possible to ensure employees will speak up honestly.

For example, while information such as a participant's department and grade are valid pieces of data (to enable micro-cultures to be identified), who specifically says what in a focus group is not valid. So while comments can be recorded, who specifically said them should not be. Being clear about this up front and adhering to it is key to increasing participation and honesty.

It is worthwhile acknowledging that not every executive team will feel comfortable undergoing this process. Such conversations need personal maturity as well as the ability to set aside defensive mechanisms and to put the good of the company ahead of one's own fears. Depending on where each member of the executive team is in relation to these elements, a body of work might need to be undertaken on an individual basis before the team is ready to engage at the group level.

The following are some suggested options available to identify actual values:

1. Executive-Team-Only Focus Group

2. Facilitated multi-level focus groups
3. One-to-one structured meetings
4. On-line survey
5. Shared technology platform

The following tables provide a description of each option and the related pros and cons, followed by any relevant notes.

Option 1   *Executive-Team-Only Focus Group*

One way to identify actual values is to facilitate an executive-team-only focus group. Using a structured process, the facilitator generates a dialogue that enables the group to express what they feel are the actual values.

+	−
Can be completed in a short period of time	Excludes insights from other levels, which often differ from executive team's
Captures executive team's perspective of the current situation	Limited by executive team's level of self-awareness, i.e., might have blind spots
Can raise awareness of the current situation among the executive team	Might be a lack of trust within group to openly admit to values perceived as "negative"
Can be used as an interim evaluation tool	Loss of opportunity to start a company-wide dialogue and engagement

Focus Group Note: A facilitated focus group should be a structured session designed to cover:

— *The purpose of the focus group*
— *What a value is*
— *Structured questions to elicit actual values and behavioral examples*
— *Time to further explore what is meant by what is being said*

Option 2   *Facilitated Multi-Level Focus Groups*

An alternate is to arrange a series of facilitated focus groups. This option provides an opportunity for employees at all levels within the company to identify what they feel the actual values are, while permitting immediate exploration of exactly what is meant by any given comment that is not clearly expressed.

— *Wider perspective so results in a more accurate picture of company's actual values— both what they are and how they manifest themselves*

— *Increases awareness and understanding of the concept of company values, increasing the likely success of the final stated values roll-out*

— *Less opportunities to hide the actual values the company doesn't want to admit to*

— *Provides a valuable source of feedback to the executive team*

— *Requires more time and resources than just an executive team focus group*

— *Depending on group dynamic, some groups may be more open and honest than others.*

Multi-Level Focus Group Notes:

i. In order to identify possible micro-cultures that have sprung up at certain grades or within specific departments, care should be taken to isolate data that might arise due to different grades and/or different departments. Depending on company and department size, this could be done by grouping together people of similar grades across departments, e.g., junior, senior, team leads, etc. It could also be achieved by grouping people of similar grades within the same department.

ii. To maintain anonymity in smaller departments, it might not be possible to isolate specific grades. Instead, employees of similar grades across several departments might be grouped together. Should strong differences of opinion arise during the focus group, the facilitator can note the relevant department, as appropriate.

For example, in many businesses, support teams such as finance, HR, and IT often only have a handful of people, e.g., three to five staff members, across a range of grades, such as head of function, manager and staff. Holding individual focus groups for each level within each department would not be feasible.

One option is to hold focus groups by grade across all these smaller functions, e.g., all staff levels, all front line managers, and/or all mid-level managers, etc. The facilitator can then make relevant notes during the focus group that, for example, in IT, x (e.g., process, technical knowledge, etc.) is more valued while in HR, y (e.g., relationships, respect, etc.) is more valued.

iii. Depending on employee numbers, the facilitated focus group method may include all employees, including an executive team focus group, or may be limited to some percentage, while ensuring sufficient representation from all departments and grades. For example, if there are fifty employees in a company, the number is small enough to be able to engage everyone. If there are two thousand, a representative sample of two to three hundred, along with the executive team, might be sufficient.

Option 3   *One-to-One Structured Meetings*

One-to-one structured meetings could be undertaken between the facilitator and pre-identified relevant employees within the company. Such individuals would include all the executive team, representation from all levels of management, and the more experienced staff members across all different departments and business units.

— *A skilled facilitator will draw out the real issues that may not come out during other formats, i.e., increased honesty and openness.*	— *Depending on staff numbers, not all staff will be included (could be overcome by using a combination of one-to-one and focus group meetings).*
— *Easier to schedule than group meetings*	— *More time-consuming and costly*
— *Removes "group think" bias*	
— *Generates a wealth of valuable insights*	
— *Increases awareness of company values, increasing chances of a successful roll-out*	

Option 4   *On-line Survey*

Create an on-line, anonymous survey that teases out the different values as perceived by different areas of the company.

+	−
— *Increasing awareness of values can increase employees' engagement, thus increasing the likelihood of support later on.*	— *Harder to further explore what some comments might mean (this could be overcome by following up with focus groups)*
— *Questions can be structured in a way that allows many of the answers to be easily collated.*	— *Survey length is limited to how long a participant will realistically spend completing it, e.g., five or ten minutes.*
— *Shorter length of time required by participants to complete survey than is needed to attend meetings*	— *Some workplaces may not be sufficiently in tune with technology, reducing the participation rate.*
— *All employees can be invited to participate.*	— *May take several hours to create an effective survey*
— *Participation rates are likely to be high in technology-driven workplaces.*	— *Survey bias might be unintentionally introduced.*
— *Surveys overcome issues of multiple office locations and/or time zone differences.*	

On-line Survey Notes:

i. The first page can be used to gather information such as grade, department, etc. This information can provide vital insight into whether there are specific teams or grades that are out of step with the company's main organizational culture.

ii. The main questions can focus on drawing out what participants feel the actual values are. Such questions might include:

1. On an everyday basis, what do you feel is focused on or is most important?

2. When it comes to making decisions, can you give three standards, behaviors, or desired results that are regularly taken into consideration as part of the decision-making process?

3. Describe the behaviors you feel are rewarded in your area.

4. Describe the behaviors you feel are rewarded within the organization.

iii. Whether as part of the survey introduction or on the main page of questions, the survey should include some explanation of what a value is, what is meant by behaviors, etc.

iv. When constructing a survey, it is important to avoid introducing a natural bias into the questions and, by extension, the answers. Rather than actually provide a list of values that people can select from, which is introducing a bias, it is better to construct the questions in a way that allows them the freedom to identify actual values. Even if participants don't actually put a name on a specific value, they can describe the behaviors they see. This will provide enough information to allow whoever is analyzing the data to recognize the trends and put names on them.

v. As part of the introduction, it is important to stress the anonymity of the responses, purpose of the exercise, who will have access to the data, what will happen to the data after the fact, etc.

Option 5   *Shared Technology Platform*

Leverage available technology to initiate an on-line, real-time conversation about the actual values, similar to IBM's approach.

(+)	(−)
— *Everyone can participate.*	— *If low levels of trust exist, participation and/or honesty likely to be low.*
— *Circumvents location and timezone issues*	— *Participation rates in technophobic companies likely to be low*
— *Points raised can be explored further immediately, possibly resulting in uncovering further relevant points.*	— *Some executives may not be able to refrain from breaking the rules of engagement, thus destroying trust in the project.*
— *Participation rates in technology-orientated companies are likely to be high.*	— *Could get very heated, resulting in frustration and employees feeling personally attacked*

Shared Technology Platform Notes:

i. This method is limited by how honest people will be. This depends on how anonymous they feel the process will really be or how likely a backlash is. If there is a culture of low trust, this option is unlikely to provide any real insights, as people will just say what they think they should say or point-blank refuse to participate.

ii. To initiate the conversation, as with other methods, explaining the purpose of the exercise, what values are, etc. should be done up front.

iii. The rules of engagement and consequences for not upholding them should also be clearly spelled out, and that *EVERYONE* will be held accountable to them. Resources should be put in place to ensure adequate monitoring and that everyone *is* actually held accountable to them.

iv. Rules of engagement should, at a minimum, cover:
  a. Whether responses are given anonymously or not
  b. If required, the purpose of the need to indicate grade and/or department, where this data will be stored, and who will have access to it (ideally, it should just be whoever is going to analyze the data)
  c. For smaller teams, if they provide their grade/department, how their anonymity will be maintained
  d. The need to show respect to all contributors, even if one employee doesn't agree with another employee's point of view
  e. Explain that as the objective is to obtain understanding, not to score points, some posts may need to be probed further, but will be done so in a positive manner.
  f. There will be no repercussions or backlash against participants.
  g. The consequences for any employee, regardless of grade, who breaks any of the rules

Data Analysis and Reporting of Findings

Regardless of which method or combination of methods is used, the data needs to be compiled, evaluated, and cross-referenced to the executive team's individual personal values, trends spotted, and actual values extracted. Ideally, this should be done by someone (or a team, depending on the volume of data gathered) who is experienced in what values are but independent of the executive team, as they're too close to the data. Once the analysis is completed, it should be shared with the executive team.

5. Evaluating the Company's Actual Values

Once the actual values are identified, the next step is to evaluate the impact and validity of each of them, individually and collectively, from the organization's perspective, and determine which values should be kept (valid values) and which need to be eased out of the workplace (comfort values).

Let's look at a company who took the time and identified that their actual values were:

— Winning
— Perfection
— Persistence
— Innovation

These values are very focused on "achieving" and there are very few of the more "touchy/feely"-type values such as respect or teamwork. While it might be uncomfortable to acknowledge that the executive team doesn't place too much emphasis on such values, the reality is that the "achieving values" are what is driving the company. To pretend otherwise by stating values at odds with these just won't make it true.

Taking a look at the executive team members' values, the common themes are:

— *Achievement*	— *Competition*
— *Perfection*	— *Determination*
— *Creativity*	— *Persistence*
— *Results*	— *Endurance*

The most striking observation that arises from looking at the above list is that they are all geared towards achieving goals without much focus on relationships or people. The feel to this workplace is that it is a high individual performance environment. It extends very little support to those who don't attain the expected standards. The high individual performance ethos tends to not extend to high performance teams, as the reward structure is designed to recognize individual performers only. This results in employees seeing others as competitors rather than collaborators.

Given our knowledge of motivation, leadership, emotional intelligence, and the importance of teamwork, this might be uncomfortable to acknowledge. However, there is strictly nothing right or wrong with this approach if the majority of employees consciously buy into it. Not only that, but there are hundreds of thousands of people in the employment market whose personal values would connect to this way of working and who would be very happy to work in this task-focused, high individual performance environment, potentially resulting in a very successful company.

Problems only arise when:

(a) the executive team doesn't want to admit to the actual values and states a conflicting set of values instead
(b) the recruitment process regularly recruits people with personal values at odds with the actual company values, diluting the actual values and causing conflict
(c) there is a sense that, while the company might be doing well, it is underperforming in relation to its potential, e.g., over-reliance on a strength (winning business, perhaps) has become a weakness (winning at all costs).

Since the executive team is aware of both the actual values and their contribution to them, they can assess if these actual values are valid for the organization's future needs, if any are damaging, or if there are any obvious gaps. Practical Guide 5.1 provides a suggested approach to setting up and conducting a facilitated evaluation workshop.

As part of preparing for the workshop, the facilitator needs to prepare a list of themes and questions to pose to the team, based on the specific set of actual values that they have already identified. Using the set of actual values identified in the example above, Table 5.1: Evaluation Workshop Sample Questions outlines many of the questions and areas a facilitator should cover during such a workshop.

Depending on the answers to the questions (and any others that arise on the day), the executive team should have a pretty clear picture about their current strengths and weaknesses. Most likely, some obvious trends and patterns will emerge.

Practical Guide 5.1

ACTUAL VALUES EVALUATION WORKSHOP

Step 1: Having already identified the company's actual values, schedule a workshop to evaluate them.

Step 2: Prior to workshop, facilitator prepares a list of themes and questions that are relevant to the set of actual values. See Table 5.1: Evaluation Workshop Sample Questions below for some ideas.

Step 3: Facilitate the workshop by enabling the group to effectively explore the impact the actual values have on the company's performance.

Step 4: Outcomes from the workshop should include: actual valid values, comfort values, and missing values.

Step 5: From the workshop, a set of final stated values should be available, consisting of actual values that have been deemed as still valid and values that have been identified as missing values. Comfort values should not be included in the final set.

Table 5.1
Evaluation Workshop Sample Questions

In relation to the example above, the executive team identified their actual company values as:

— *Winning*
— *Perfection*
— *Persistence*
— *Innovation*

Questions and themes the facilitator should cover during the actual values evaluation workshop include:

— **In relation to ranking values:**
  — *How are the values currently ranked?*
  — *What is the impact of ranking them in this order?*
  — *Would there be a different cultural impact if they were ranked differently?*
  — *Is the ranking consistent or does it vary depending on the decision or situation?*

— **In relation to the value of perfection:**
  — *Is 100 percent demanded for every task done?*
  — *Do all tasks need to be completed to a standard of 100 percent?*
  — *Do all employees share the value of perfection?*
  — *If not, what percentage doesn't and what is the impact of consistently demanding such a high standard from them?*
  — *Is this negatively impacting team or business performance?*
  — *Are opportunities being missed by these people not contributing?*

— **In relation to the value of winning:**
  — *Are we winning at the cost of our relationships?*
  — *Do we brow-beat our customers into saying yes, even when they don't want to?*

Table 5.1 (cont.)
Evaluation Workshop Sample Questions

— *What is the short-term impact of that?*
— *What is the long-term impact of that?*
— *Do we develop one-way or two-way relationships (with clients, employees, third parties)?*
— *If we haven't, how is this impacting our relationships?*
— *Do we listen to our customers, employees, third parties?*
— *Could we perform better if we listened more closely and honestly evaluate the feedback?*
— *Are we actually underperforming, even though we think we're winning?*

— **In relation to the value of persistence:**
  — *Is our persistence a strength?*
  — *Does it enable us to keep striving for improved, innovative products (or services)?*
  — *Do we go too far with persistence?*
  — *Can this blind-side us into it becoming a weakness at times?*

— **In relation to the impact of combining winning and persistence:**
  — *Can we go too far with persistence when combined with winning?*
  — *Are we working as a team or do we try to out-do and out-win each other?*
  — *Do we need to work as a team or is individual performance sufficient?*
  — *If so, what impact is this having down the line?*
  — *Is the impact making our work lives easier or harder?*

— **In relation to overall impact of the combined actual values:**
  — *Is the combination of these four values sustainable long term or do people burn out?*
  — *What are our staff turnover figures like?*

Table 5.1 (cont.)
Evaluation Workshop Sample Questions

— *Are we developing excellent levels of knowledge and expertise, only to consistently lose it as people leave?*

— *Is there a specific pattern as to when we lose people and their expertise, e.g., is there a certain point in people's lives when they seem to leave? After a certain number of years?*

— *If so, what is the cost of this to the company?*

— *What are the benefits of this combination of values?*

— *Do the benefits outweigh the costs?*

— *How can we balance our values so that they work for us, not against us?*

— *What is our customer attrition rate like?*

— *Is that rate desirable or acceptable?*

— *What are the causes of the attrition rate?*

— *Are any of these values in natural conflict with another?*

— *Have any of our values become overly used?*

— *If so, has it become a weakness?*

— **Exploring expendable values:**

— *What one value would you dump?*

— *What difference do you think dumping this value would make?*

— *Is there another value you would dump and what difference do you think it would make?*

— *If you dumped one of these, what do you think it should be replaced with? For what reasons?*

— **Exploring missing values:**

— *What values do you feel are key to the long-term future success of the company? For what reasons?*

— *Given our group common preferences, how likely is it that we could support each of these proposed values?*

— *Which missing values (if any) are we going to include in our final stated values?*

— *What behaviors would support such missing values?*

For example, it could turn out that winning is causing some issues with employees' abilities to build relationships and to collaborate effectively, both internally and externally, resulting in lost opportunities and underperformance. Again, perfection might be de-motivating many employees, particularly when coupled with a high competitive environment with low support, generated by the value of winning. A big question for the company is whether these trends are strengths or if they have become weaknesses.

Such learning is not very pleasant and might well be very painful but ignoring it doesn't change the reality of what is happening. Many executive teams resist undertaking such a review, often out of fear of what opening the can of worms will result in. However, as when an executive undergoes self-reflection and learning during the coaching process, undergoing such organizational reflection and learning leads to a clearer understanding of the company's strengths and weaknesses and permits a more considered solution to be implemented. Again, the need to do this was strongly highlighted in Jim Collins' book *Good to Great*.

Finally, referring back to the point that sometimes organizational cultures retain the impact of personal values from previous executives, if there is no correlation between the current incumbents' values and the actual values, it might be worthwhile considering if any departed executive members held values that would underpin the actual values and explain where they originated from. Such a scenario allows more of a blank slate to design more appropriate final stated values.

Number of Final Stated Values

Once the actual values evaluation has been completed, the company's list of final stated values is now ready. While there is no absolute number of values a company should have, best practice would suggest that the number should be kept around five. For any company to consistently uphold five values would, in itself, be a pretty impressive feat. If the list of final stated values contains more than five or six, an executive/senior management team workshop could be held to rank them in order of importance and settle on what the final five or six are.

6. Defining Final Stated Values

At this point, there is a set of final stated values. However, before these can be communicated and rolled out throughout the organization, there are a few additional steps that need to be undertaken by the executive team to increase the prospect of successfully implementing them.

If the final stated values have not already been defined in detail as part of previous steps, then it is best to define them at this time. As we saw from the marketing director example, what commonly happens is that the value names are identified without any explanation or understanding as to what they mean in everyday terms. Even for some companies that do define their values, they define them in such narrow terms that they are too inflexible and so lose their effectiveness.

For example, take a company that values respect and defines it as follows:

> *We treat all our customers with dignity and respect. We consider their needs and endeavor to deliver them, while managing natural constraints.*

Defining respect in this way puts an onus on all employees to treat customers with respect without extending the concept of respect to internal staff. Staff may well become cynical as they experience the discrepancy between their being expected to treat customers with respect while, behind closed doors, they are shouted at or treated in other disrespectful ways. If respect is worth valuing and upholding, surely it is worth valuing consistently, across the board, with everyone, not just as and when it suits. By the executive team taking the time to discuss this, such issues can be highlighted and definitions adjusted accordingly.

Options to Increase Understanding of Final Stated Values

It is important for the executive team to consider what each value means and what groups of people it might impact upon, as well as how different areas of the business might interpret and rank them.

The more discussion that is had about what each value means and what behaviors support each one in practice, the better the executive team is able to model them. In addition, they are better positioned to initiate conversations around behaviors that don't uphold the values and provide guidance as to how actions and decisions might be reframed in terms of them.

While this clearly requires a big commitment from the team, the time taken to gain an in-depth understanding of the meaning and scope of each value really pays dividends down the road. The greater the cohesion between the executive team, in their understanding of the final stated values, the meaning of each of them, and their applications, the greater the likelihood of successfully incorporating them into the company's way of doing business. If the executive team is really serious about introducing active company values, it's a step that should not be skipped.

Two suggested approaches are outlined in Practical Guides 5.2 and 5.3. Regardless of the approach taken, once the executive team is confident that they fully understand the meaning of each final stated value, the definitions should be reviewed and updated accordingly.

Practical Guide 5.2

EXAMPLES OF SUPPORTING VALUES

Step 1: Executive team has initial discussion of the meaning of each value. The findings are written up and distributed to all participants.

Step 2: Allow content to sit with participants for a few days/ weeks, while they think further on the meaning of each value.

Step 3: Set an exercise to ask everyone to bring two examples for each value to the next meeting—the first example to illustrate behavior that honors the value and the second example to illustrate behavior that breaches it. If bringing ten or twelve examples (assuming five or six values) to the next meeting is considered too much, then assign two values per executive that they need to find examples for.

Step 4: Discuss these examples at the next meeting. These examples provide excellent real-life opportunities to examine the values further and deepen everyone's understanding.

Practical Guide 5.3

LIVING THE VALUES ASSESSMENT

Step 1: At the end of each executive meeting, take out the list of final stated values and ask the group to assess how well they did at "Living the Values" during the meeting.

Step 2: Depending on the level of honesty and trust within the team, step one can be done directly through dialogue or indirectly by rating each value on a form with space to allow supporting evidence to be provided.

Step 3: Determine the average rating for each value.

Step 4: For values that receive a low rating, allocate ten minutes to discuss why the group feels that the specific value was not being honored, using supporting evidence as the starting point of the discussion. Such discussions should be framed in neutral language to prevent individuals feeling attacked.

Step 5: These steps should be repeated after each meeting until the consensus is that each final stated value is being regularly honored.

Clash between Executive Personal Values and Final Stated Values

Having finalized the company values and their definitions, an obvious question that arises is:

> *What happens if, upon agreeing on the final stated values, a member of the executive team feels that, in all consciousness, they are not in a position to uphold and support them?*

An executive who no longer fits into a company's revised approach to business cannot realistically remain and actively support it. So, the only real option is for him or her to move on. As highlighted in Key Concept 4.7, it's important to recognize that this is not personal on either side and, again, neither is right or wrong— just different perspectives.

While this might seem a draconian response, it must be remembered that for most industries and most jobs, there are many different companies supplying the same products and/or services or having need of similar roles (e.g., HR, IT, finance, etc.). As with this company, each has their own approach as to how they deliver their purpose. The executive in question is more than likely to share their values with at least one of these other companies. Assisting them to find such an organization and provide the support they need to move on, both physically and emotionally, enables the relationship to end amicably and minimize the reputational damage, while retaining trust internally.

As part of such a conversation, it should be highlighted to executives who find themselves in this position that there is nothing personal in this. A key point to stress to them is that the proposed change is sufficiently different to what is important to them, i.e., to their own personal values, that they will find it very difficult to settle in to the new way, resulting in their feeling at odds with the company going forward. It is as equally in their interest as the company's that they move on as easily and painlessly as possible.

The last word on this topic goes to former CEO of GE, Jack Welch. In his book *Winning*, he makes the point that if a company is serious about walking their values talk, they need to *"reward the people who exhibit them and 'punish' those that don't."* He goes on to say that *"every time we asked one of our high-performing managers to leave because he didn't demonstrate the values—and we said as much publicly—the organization responded incredibly well."* GE is well known for its belief in and active support of upholding company values and regularly features in Fortune 500's list of top ten companies.

7. Ranking Final Stated Values

Before moving on to the implementation phase, as suggested in the reducing conflict strategies section, the final step is for the executive team to determine the order in which they rank the values. Take, for example, a company with the following values:

— *Doing the Right Thing*
— *Trust and Teamwork*
— *Winning*

Without trying very hard, it's easy to envision a conflict arising between doing the right thing and winning, during a potential sale. For example, a potential client might inquire about different ways to get a body of work done and suggest ways that are not 100 percent above board. Which values becomes more important?

Is it more important to "win" the business or is it more important to risk losing the business while upholding the right way to complete the work? How the values are ranked impacts the company's preferred approach to be taken and provides additional guidance to the salesperson.

Or what about a situation where an operations team is behind schedule to deliver a piece of work but they want to be seen as winning? Is it okay to start cutting corners and standards or should they uphold the integrity of the work and miss the deadline?

Reasons to Pre-Rank Company Values

Rather than waiting for such a situation to arise, it is more effective for the executive team to consider what the ranking order is in a calm, clear-thinking manner, not when faced with the additional pressure of an actual situation.

Some executive teams might conclude that ranking order would depend on the situation and that it should be determined on a case-by-case basis. It's worthwhile to be aware of and consider the possible consequences that might arise from such an approach.

First, if the executive team is not clear about the ranking order, how can other employees be sure in what order they should apply the values when such a situation arises?

Second, such an approach relies on the relevant employee or department escalating the situation up to the executive team. This may or may not happen.

Third, the need to escalate each situation slows the decision down, potentially resulting in lost opportunities.

Fourth, not having a consistent approach to applying the ranking order leaves the executive team open to criticism and, as we saw in the chapter on conflict, could generate a source of organizational conflict. In a situation where employees feel that the values were ranked in the wrong way, it may result in a breach of trust and cynicism. The more open and transparent the executive team is, the more effective the use of values will be.

If the decision is made to still not openly rank the final stated values, it is wise to at least acknowledge that such situations will arise and that the ranking to be applied will be discussed at the time. This option allows for required flexibility while minimizing potential damage. As with all such communications, though, when such a situation actually does arise, it's important to follow through and ensure that the appropriate ranking is considered and clearly communicated.

If a ranking is not offered, it is advisable to consider the likelihood of teams implicitly ranking the values from their perspective.

As we saw in the chapter on conflict, given that such implicit rankings can lead to inter-team conflict, this should be taken into consideration when making the decision to not issue a company-wide ranking order.

An alternative approach is for each department to rank the company values as applicable to them and make this information available throughout the organization. They can then become a point of reference for other departments, reducing the likelihood of inter-team conflict, increasing awareness of other departments' needs, and increasing co-operation.

Effective Company Values

Earlier on, we saw that many companies introduce values as single words, with no interpretation provided, and we also saw how values definitions can be too narrowly defined, both of which can cause problems at the implementation stage. To finish off this section, let's look at elements that contribute to creating effective company values. As we saw earlier, some typical company values are:

Integrity, Respect, Honesty, Diversity, Customer Focus, Innovation, and Performance

— An effective company value goes beyond the obvious and captures elements that go before some of these generic values. For example, if the generic value is customer focus, what is it about the customers' needs that the company is focused on exactly? Is it their money? Or is it the customer's level of satisfaction with their interaction with the company? Is it looking for the best solution to the customer's needs, even if that means another company is better positioned to meet them? Or is it designing the experience from the customer's experience, not the company's internal processes? Explicitly pinpointing the way in which the company wants to focus on the customer provides a more unique company value than the usual "customer focus."

— An effective company value definition is open enough to apply to everyone, internal and external to the organization. Looking at the example of respect defined above, we saw that it was defined in terms of the customer only. To be effective, it should apply to everyone and not only to one group of people, in this case, the customer. In contrast, IBM's value, trust, and personal responsibility in all relationships is expressed in such a way that it clearly indicates that all relationships matter, not just the one with the client.

— For a company value that can easily be interpreted in positional terms, e.g., fairness, the definition should clearly recognize that it is applied from all parties' perspectives, including the organization's, not just from an individual's perspective.

— Consideration could also be given to which personal values might map over to and support a company value. For example, innovation is a very common corporate value, so what personal values might underpin it? Curiosity, discovery, adaptability, flexibility, and inquisitiveness are some values that would naturally feed into and support such a value.

Chapter Five Summary

— *Taking time to determine the current actual values that are in play, even if it is uncomfortable to acknowledge them, increases the successful introduction of new or revised company values.*

— *Each member of the executive team should be aware of their own personal values and how they support or clash with the company's final stated values.*

— *An analysis of the actual values, splitting them into valid and comfort values, can be undertaken, along with identifying missing values. The final stated values are then made up of a combination of valid and missing values.*

— *Creating common meanings, definitions, and rankings for each final stated value increases the likelihood of their being upheld and applied across the company on a consistent basis.*

— *Executives who feel they can't actively support the final stated values can be assisted in moving on.*

CHAPTER SIX

Implementing Final Stated Values

Now that the company values are finalized, the next step is to introduce them to the wider organization and to implement them.

Recapping the list outlined in the previous chapter, we covered points one to seven.

Recap

1. What company values are and are not
2. The difference between "stated" values and "actual" values
3. What the executive team's personal values are
4. What the company's actual values are
5. Evaluating the company's actual values
6. Defining final stated values
7. Ranking final stated values
8. Ways the executive team needs to uphold the final stated values
9. How to communicate values throughout the company
10. How to incorporate values into daily business

This chapter will focus on the remaining three areas:

8. Ways the executive team needs to uphold the final stated values
9. How to communicate the final stated values throughout the company
10. How to incorporate the final stated values into daily business

8. Upholding and Supporting Final Stated Values

The executive team needs to be confidently aware that they are regularly upholding and modeling the final stated values, before they start communicating them on a wider basis.

As outlined in Practical Guide 5.3, one suggestion is that at the end of every executive meeting, even if it's a meeting between two or three executive members, they could take out the values and rate how well they feel they did in demonstrating each of them and make suggestions as to how they could better uphold them.

It could be agreed up front that this exercise will be done for a specific period of time, e.g., one month, two months (depending on how regularly the group meets and how many new values are being introduced), with the findings and observations being noted and discussed for the benefit of all.

During this phase, particular emphasis should be placed on the missing values being introduced and, specifically, how well they are being supported. Since a huge behavioral shift is required in order to support this new sub-set of values, greater vigilance and reflection is needed to ensure the executive team is actively supporting the change. Failure to make the shift at this level will undermine success when rolling the values out to the wider organization, resulting in wasted time and effort and the loss of benefits that actively living the values can bring.

There is a direct relationship between the number of missing values identified and the length of time the executive team should take during this step. For example, introducing two new values will take longer to embed than one. While the team might be anxious to move on to the next step of rolling out the values, this new set is going to be around for a long time so there's no hurry in taking an extra month or two to get it right.

Another approach is to start communicating the ideas to the next one to two levels of management. Doing a semi-dry run of explaining the concepts, the steps that were undertaken, what the final stated values are, their meanings, and the awareness, gleaned to date, of how to honor them would provide valuable learning for the executive team and enable the next level(s) down to start engaging with and implementing them, too.

Acknowledgement of the comfort values and related behaviors could also be shared with this group, along with the message that these are being phased out and will no longer be tolerated. Such a conversation should describe: the comfort values; examples of behaviors and decisions that highlight how they had been upheld in the organization; how such behaviors and decisions will no longer be acceptable; and examples of the missing values that they should be replaced with.

Regardless of the approach taken, the executive team should feel comfortable with what the final stated values are, what they mean, how they are to be used in everyday life, and that they are actively applying them daily before communicating them throughout the organization.

9. Communicating Final Stated Values

The next step is to communicate the final stated values throughout the business. Very few companies manage to over-communicate any message but the vast majority regularly manage to *under-communicate* messages.

That said, there is a balance to be struck between the initial communication/awareness-raising and ongoing communication. Oftentimes, companies focus a huge amount of effort in communicating the message initially and then it drops off a cliff. Executives assume it's been implemented, so they don't need to worry about it anymore, while employees assume it's been swallowed up by the "initiatives black hole" and won't be back to bother them any time in the near future. Instead, a steady and consistent communication plan will win the day.

When designing a communication strategy, care should be given to the following phases:

— *Initial launch*
— *Initial roll-out*
— *Ongoing values focus*

Phase 1: Initial Launch

The size of the organization and the number of offices/locations/time zones it works across will influence the approach taken to initially communicate the final values.

For example, some large multi-nationals are adept at holding "town-hall" type meetings, where employees can dial or video conference in to listen/watch the CEO address the whole organization simultaneously. For small businesses, getting all the staff together in a room is more feasible. For other company types and sizes, the solution will lie somewhere in between.

Whatever the right solution is for a given company, the key thing is for the message to be delivered in person and that it is clearly communicated and explained. Elements to consider covering in such a presentation are outlined in Table 6.1: Final Stated Values Initial Launch Content.

Many larger companies communicate messages in person, from the CEO to the senior management team, who, in turn, communicate it down to their teams. Much of the message can be lost in translation, particularly when interpreted through each manager's personal values filters. This inevitably results in mixed messages and/or incomplete delivery.

Table 6.1
Final Stated Values Initial Launch Content

— *What company values are*
— *The purpose and role company values play within the company*
— *How values underpin the company's vision and mission statement*
— *Explain the different categories of values, i.e., actual, stated, valid, etc.*
— *The process the executive team went through to determine the final stated values. For example,*
   ○ *Actual values identified*
   ○ *Comfort and valid values*
   ○ *Missing values*
   ○ *Final stated values*
— *The final stated values and their meanings, as agreed by the executive team*
— *The role all employees will play in teasing them out further, particularly in relation to each value's boundaries*
— *The behavioral shift that will be required to support the final stated values, particularly to support the missing values and to phase out the comfort values*
— *The need to rank values and the company's ranking of them (or a caveat that rankings will be considered at the time of a conflict, if relevant)*
— *The mechanisms that are going to be put in place to raise "values awareness" across the company and the executive team's expectations around integration*
— *How the final stated values will be integrated into everyday processes, e.g., performance management, decision-making, recruitment, etc.*
— *The consequences of not living up to the final stated values*
— *Options available to employees who feel they can't support the final stated values*

To ensure consistency of message, this initial communication should be delivered to all staff members, at all levels, by the CEO. If that's not feasible due to workforce size, location, time zones, etc., delivery should be split among the executive team. This ensures that the initial message is delivered by someone who was part of the whole process and is able to answer any questions that arise, especially questions around the required behavioral changes, how they will be supported, and the consequences of not supporting them.

If the initial communication is being split among the executive team, one suggestion is that in preparation for the launch meetings, the team brainstorms the types of questions that might arise, including all the "elephants in the room" type of questions, and agree on honest, consistent answers to each of them. During the initial roll-out meetings, if no one is brave or comfortable enough to ask about the elephants[13], the executive should address them anyway, since there's an agreed-on set of answers available. By doing so, it sends out a strong message that there is nothing to hide.

Phase 2: Initial Roll-Out

Once the initial launch is complete, the next phase is the initial roll-out. While all employees attended an initial launch meeting, they now need time to consider and tease out exactly what the final stated values mean to them, their role, their team, and across the company.

As part of the initial launch, clear guidelines should have been given in relation to the mechanisms to be put in place to raise awareness and understanding across the company and the executive team's expectations around integration. Ideally, this should include outlining mechanisms and expectations in relation to enabling dialogue, dealing with queries, concerns, or questions that arise, how to share answers on valid points or common questions that arise and haven't already been addressed, regularity of dialogue, and timeframes (e.g., to hold dialogues, to answer questions,

---

13 While each organization will have their own elephants, some examples might include: previous experience of actions not matching words; or an actual value that has clearly not been named.

to share knowledge, to start seeing behavioral change, for values to be integrated into processes, decision-making, etc.).

Suggested Initial Roll-Out Approaches

While there is any number of ways to address all of the above, the most important point to keep at the forefront is the overall objective of ensuring that people start engaging with and living the final stated values. The starting point to achieve this objective is to generate an understanding of what is expected of them. This can be done either in person or electronically, using one or more of the following suggested approaches:

Approach 1: Team workshops
Approach 2: Small businesses
Approach 3: On-line

Approach 1: Team Workshops

This approach, suitable for mid-size to large organizations, is for dialogue to be generated by managers at all levels within the company by holding values workshop with their team, starting from the top. As with all change, it is vital that the executive team is actively seen as part of this roll-out. Their involvement is two-fold: first, at this point, they are the ones with the most in-depth understanding of what the final stated values mean; second, it actively shows their commitment to supporting them.

Depending on the number of layers of management, locations, team sizes, etc., the practical implementation runs the gamut. In one company, the executive of each function might be the one to hold the structured team meeting with the whole department to discuss the values, as outlined above. This minimizes the likelihood of miscommunication and misunderstanding but may not be feasible in larger organizations.

In another company, a cascade approach could be taken, with the executive member holding a structured team meeting with their senior management team. Once all queries and questions arising from that meeting are answered and distributed across the senior management team, each senior manager is then responsible for holding a structured team meeting with their teams.

Approach 2: Small Business

For a small company, a more appropriate approach would be for the CEO to chair such a meeting with all staff members in attendance. This way, all questions and concerns are answered straight away and everyone hears the same message.

Approach 3: On-line

For companies that have a strong on-line culture, they could use technology to generate the dialogue on-line. An obvious disadvantage to this is that there is no guarantee that people will engage with or read the information. However, on the plus side, for those that do engage, the executive team knows they really are interested and want to know more.

Initial Roll-Out Objectives

Regardless of the approach(es) taken, the overall objectives of this step is to ensure that all employees discuss the following:

— *Meanings of each of the final stated values and their associated behaviors*
— *Boundaries of each value, i.e., what they do and don't mean*
— *Impact of each value to their team and their relationships with other teams*
— *Obvious potential conflicts, both internally and with other teams*
— *Impact of values on decision-making within and across teams*

No matter which approach is taken to generate the dialogue, some points that can be easily overlooked or forgotten during such a process are outlined in Table 6.2: Initial Roll-Out Points to Remember.

Table 6.2
Initial Roll-Out Points to Remember

— *The purpose is to generate dialogue in order to consider what the values really mean. The more they are discussed and considered, the clearer the consistent interpretation.*

— *The executive and senior management teams should be open to engaging in honest conversation. They should not take comments personally nor should they shut down comments that they don't like. To do so would seriously undermine the success of the whole process.*

— *In the case of holding meetings, make them fun. Even if fun isn't one of the final stated values, make it a fun, interesting, engaging experience, not drudgery. Have it off-site, make a morning or day of it, have prizes for the silliest, funniest, most complex, best contribution and/or most imaginative example, or any other category that can be thought of.*

— *Consider ways to actively start upholding some of the final stated values as part of the dialogue process. For example, if creativity makes the list, ask the team to draw up a list of rules to be applied during the meeting that upholds creativity. Put someone in charge of counting how many times each person upheld or failed to uphold those rules. Check in every so often so people are getting real-time feedback during the meeting. Have a prize for the person who upholds the rules the most consistently, who improves the most, etc.*

— *Permit and encourage people to challenge, in a non-aggressive way. They should challenge each others' assumptions, beliefs, personal values, specific meanings etc.*

All queries, questions, or concerns that arise as part of the dialogue and cannot be clearly answered should be noted, to be considered and answered at a later date. Again, how this is done is up to each company. In a smaller company, where the CEO conducted the meeting in the first place, it is unlikely that many questions will be outstanding. In larger companies, such queries should be brought back to the executive team to be considered collectively, with the resultant answers clearly communicated.

Even if a shared technology platform hadn't been used initially, using it as this point could allow queries and answers to be posted very effectively.

Such a platform also permits an ongoing dialogue to be maintained. For example, three months down the line, should a situation arise that hadn't been previously considered, the relevant manager or team could post the query and seek opinions as to how best to deal with it while upholding the values.

As outlined in Practical Guide 6.1, indicative timeframes should be put in place to ensure the dialogue stage doesn't become all talk with no action. A timeline indicating "initial dialogue" stage, "queries posed and answered" stage, "follow-up dialogue" stage, and "live" stage should be published.

If this seems all just a little too much work and not necessary, let's revisit the IBM story. They held their original on-line discussion in 2003, which enabled them to not only identify their actual values but also allowed them to agree on their final stated values, as we saw in the chapter on identifying company values. However, in 2004, they held a second on-line discussion, focused this time on identifying and sharing ways they could actively uphold and support behaviors that sustained their core values. In effect, they recognized that it wasn't enough to just identify their core values but that they also needed to spend time identifying how they were going to support them.

SAMPLE VALUES ROLL-OUT TIMELINES

Initial Dialogue Stage: two to four weeks

Questions Posed Stage: one to two weeks

Questions Answered Stage: one to two weeks

Follow-Up Dialogue Stage: two to three weeks

Live Date: date the values are considered live

Period from Initial Dialogue to Live Stage: six to eleven weeks

Note: The suggested time ranges allow for employee numbers. For larger organizations, it might take up to four weeks to hold all the necessary initial workshops.

Phase 3: Ongoing Values Focus

Once the initial values roll-out is completed, how can the company maintain an ongoing dialogue? Intuitively, if these values have been identified as so important to the company's philosophy of doing business, it stands to reason that they should be at the forefront of people's minds, actions, interactions, and decisions.

Ongoing Values Focus Options

While there are many different ways to maintain focus on the values, here are some suggestions that might be helpful.

Option 1: On-line forum
Option 2: Regular group meetings
Option 3: Values guide
Option 4: Values program

Option 1: On-line Forum

Given the widespread availability of technology, one support mechanism might be to have some sort of on-line space dedicated to teasing out examples and situations, with input and thoughts supplied by, among others, the executive team. By actively seeing them participate in the ongoing dialogue, it clearly indicates to employees that this isn't just another passing fad to be promptly forgotten by "the powers that be" but is expected to be implemented by everyone else.

Option 2: Regular Group Meetings

Another option is to have regular group meetings, with the relevant executive(s) in attendance, to discuss what the values are, to reflect on examples of how they have been implemented, highlight examples of where they were ignored, and identify ways they can be more actively supported. This type of meeting should also regularly take place among the CEO, the executive team, and the senior management team (if relevant).

How often is "regular"? For some organizations, there might be an obvious "regular" meeting that naturally supports a values slot. In other workplaces, this might not be the case and neither does the culture lend itself to such meetings. These businesses will need to make a conscious decision to define "regular."

At the beginning, meetings probably need to be every month, particularly in cases where two or more missing values are being introduced and/or one or two comfort values are being phased out. This can then gradually be reduced down to quarterly.

Option 3: Values Guide

As part of the initial roll-out stage, many behaviors and possible conflict situations will have been identified by different departments and teams. Rather than let all this incredibly valuable material languish somewhere or become lost, it could be gathered and compiled into useful guidelines and made available to all. Such a guide would be particularly useful for explaining final stated values to new employees. It can be made available either on-line or in hard copy, e.g., as part of an employee handbook or as a company document.

Option 4: Values Program

The final suggestion is to create a twelve-month values program, designed to discuss specific issues or topics on a monthly basis. It could be conducted either on-line or emailed to relevant managers, to be discussed within each department with findings, suggestions, and questions sent back to a central co-ordinator. Relevant information could then be fed into subsequent months' content.

Alternatively, it could be converted into a twenty-four-month plan, with discussion points raised every second month and the findings and answers to questions disseminated every other month.

Finally, if the following point hasn't been stressed enough, let's stress it once more: one of the keys to successfully introducing meaningful company values is the need for all the executives to walk the talk. If none of the executives are actively seen to support them, they really will make a nice wall plaque but be of little practical use, resulting in lost opportunities, increased conflict, and underperformance.

10. Incorporating Final Stated Values into Daily Business

By this stage, the initial rolling out of company values has been completed and the awareness-raising process has come to a natural end. The values have gone live. Some obvious questions at this stage are:

— *How do the values become embedded into the company's culture?*
— *What are the consequences if the values aren't upheld?*
— *How does the company ensure that turnover and growth in staff numbers don't dilute or change the values?*

Embedding Final Stated Values

As we have seen above, the process undertaken so far has already generated a huge number of behavioral examples and possible conflict situations that can be used as guidelines. Company-wide dialogue has already increased awareness, but how can the company protect itself against the loss or dilution of this knowledge?

The expected behaviors need to be actively integrated into the company's performance, recruitment, and talent management processes. People need to understand that not only will their performance be assessed by "what" they achieve, i.e., their results, but also by "how" they achieve it, i.e., by how well they uphold the final stated values.

It's worth reiterating here that the final stated values make up a part of the company's mission statement, so the company is communicating to its customers that not only are they going to achieve X (the outcomes), they are going to do so by focusing on A, B, and C (the values). Not only will employees' performance be assessed on how well they uphold the values, but it should account for a large part of their performance, probably in the region of 40 to 60 percent. For a company that has traditionally focused on evaluating performance based only on results, this will feel very uncomfortable, but to not do so sends out a signal that company values aren't really *that* important after all.

The need to uphold the company values should also be integrated into the company's approach to talent management. Promoting employees who do not actively uphold the company values completely undermines the message of how important they are. Such promotions allow employees to see a different set of behaviors being "rewarded." This will result in their imitating those behaviors, regardless of how much talk has gone into explaining the final stated values. In addition, a huge amount of conflict and cynicism will be needlessly generated, as we saw in the chapter on conflict.

This means that if a superstar is great at getting results but in a manner incompatible with the company's final stated values, this needs to be actively managed, sooner rather than later. An honest conversation needs to be had, clearly highlighting how their behaviors are not upholding the company values and what needs to change. If there is a persistent refusal to engage with and support the values, a discussion, similar to that outlined in Practical Guide 4.3 for an executive, should be had.

The main difference between to the two conversations is that, for a superstar that has yet to rise sufficiently high up the ranks, the conversation should focus on the impact that not upholding the values will have on their career within the company. This gives them the opportunity to assess their options and what best suits them, before too much damage is done.

While such a conversation might be uncomfortable, it doesn't change the need to have it. The alternative is to land right back at square one. The more senior the person, the more crucial this conversation becomes.

Consequences of Not Upholding Final Values

People need to very clearly understand and actively see the consequences of not upholding the company's final stated values. This is where actions really do need to match words.

It's up to each company to define suitable consequences but, at a minimum, the obvious ones include:

— *One-to-one meetings to provide feedback on how a person's behavior or decisions are not upholding the values*
— *Low performance ratings actually being given to people who don't uphold the values, even if they have achieved their outcome-based objectives*
— *People who consistently don't uphold the values not being promoted*
— *Bonuses cut to match low performance ratings*

Preventing Dilution of Company Values due to New Staff

Finally, in order to ensure that new staff members, particularly at senior and executive levels, don't dilute the company values culture achieved, it's important to actively recruit new staff whose personal values underpin and dovetail with them. Focusing on hiring people who have both the skills and abilities required for a given role plus the personal values that complement the company's final stated values ensures they become self-sustaining. This reduces the likelihood of conflict, increases the probability of a successful hire, and reduces the likelihood of performance issues arising.

Chapter Six Summary

— *Final stated values need to be upheld in deed as well as in word.*

— *Clear communication is required around what the final stated values are, what they mean, and how they will be used.*

— *Engage in an ongoing dialogue to raise everyone's awareness.*

— *Guidelines can be developed to show practical application of final stated values.*

— *Clearly communicate the consequences of not upholding the final stated values and ensure such consequences are put into action for those who don't, starting from the top.*

CHAPTER SEVEN

Embedding Company Values

The really hard stuff is done: a set of final stated values has been thrashed out, they've been rolled out throughout the organization, all the necessary difficult conversations have taken place, and there is a tangible sense that behaviors and decision-making have shifted towards upholding the values. Now what?

If a company is saying that their values are a key way in how they approach achieving their business objectives, then they need to be protected and upheld on a daily basis. The final step is to incorporate related behaviors into organizational processes. This chapter will take a look at five specific areas they can be integrated and embedded into:

1. *Recruitment*
2. *Decision-Making*
3. *Marketing and Branding*
4. *Performance Management*
5. *Leadership Development*

1. Company Values and Recruitment

While working with Joan, a small business owner, it came to light that she constantly had problems with her employees. Staff turnover was relatively high and Joan often ended up in low-level conflict situations with staff members.

As part of our work, we identified Joan's personal values. I then asked her to compare these values to the behaviors she saw in her staff. It became abundantly evident that, while the employees had the "skills" to do the job and the same interest in customer care, they didn't share Joan's value of commercialism. This resulted in a negative effect on the viability of the business and a continuous low-level of conflict between Joan and her team. We went on to discuss the importance of finding people who could not only do the job but also shared Joan's values. As staff left, Joan focused her recruitment on both skills and values and selected employees who had similar values as herself. When I caught up with Joan two years later, she was much happier with her team and found herself spending a lot less time fretting over and trying to "manage" them and more time focused on new business opportunities. Life had become easier for her.

Many companies recruit for skills, knowledge, and experience, and overlook how a person's values connect to the company's values. From my experience of working with managers, the common "ouch" point for them is "how" a staff member does something. It is rarely getting the task done that is the problem; it is inevitably how they approach doing it, i.e., the behaviors they exhibit while doing it.

In a company that values initiative, recruiting a person who values resourcefulness, taking initiative, or problem-solving would nicely connect to the organization's approach to achieving results. They will connect with the manager and team a lot better than someone who values conformity or safety.

In a workplace that values teamwork and respect, a sales manager needs to recruit a salesperson with values such as courtesy, empathy, or inclusiveness, values that acknowledge and support the collective team contribution required to generate and support a sale, from start to finish. In contrast, a salesperson who values results, independence, and personal ambition might be a lone player and would be better suited to a sales team that values that approach. While both approaches bring in sales, a salesperson using the wrong approach as per the company's perspective can wreak havoc.

When it comes down to it, the easiest thing in the world is to train a person for knowledge and skills. The hardest thing in the world is to "train" a person for values. They either are of a similar mindset and outlook or they're not. This translates into my recruitment motto: recruit for values; train for skills.

No matter how I have sliced and diced "management" and the underlying keys to getting it right, it inevitably comes back to the importance of recruiting the most suitable people *for your company's needs*, whatever they are. Getting this right makes everyone's life so much easier. Getting it wrong is hell on earth due to the amount of management time spent dealing with problems arising from a poor recruitment choice.

While many companies take the skills element seriously, through use of ability tests, and some have introduced competency-based interviews and/or personality assessment tools, very few businesses explicitly recruit for values. For those companies that do effectively use competency-based behavioral indicators to recruit, the more closely aligned these indicators are to their values behaviors, the better the fit will be, due to the cross-over.

The upshot of all this is that, for many companies, rather than taking the extra time up front to get the right person, they end up spending 80 percent of their management time actively managing 20 percent of the staff who are delivering 20 percent of the results. That, of course, is assuming they do actually deal with the performance issues, since many managers take the head-in-the-sand approach, hoping it will all go away. The best-case scenario is that the person leaves of their own accord in a relatively short timeframe. In the worst-case scenario, the costs[14], such as a drop in morale and performance, attention focused on the wrong things, conflict, and disintegrating trust, start mounting up and the company starts losing its best people.

---

14 For a more in-depth list of costs that arise from poor hiring decisions, please see www.irialofarrell.com.

While it is important to recruit people, at all levels, with similar values, it becomes even more crucial at the senior manager and executive levels, as they directly impact the company's active upholding of the values. If people at this level are recruited or promoted with personal values that conflict with the company's final stated values, conflict will raise its ugly head and all the hard work will be undone.

Returning to my anecdote about the first piece of values work I undertook, when the CEO refused to implement the agreed-on company values, there was a bit more to the story. About a year prior, there had been a small acquisition whereby the company acquired a small business unit, along with the employees, from another company. About five of them were placed into relatively senior positions. During the following year, and in the timeframe of my wider project, about three to four of the original executives moved on and many of these five senior staff were promoted to the executive team, including the new CEO.

Unsurprisingly, many of these new executives were of a similar mindset to each other and of a noticeably different mindset than the incumbent team. So, what was happening during the workshop was the emergence of the two competing sets of values. As originally noted, numbers won the battle on the day but lost the war. Ultimately, while there was a sufficient number of incumbent executives to outvote the newer executives, the CEO was from the newer group and vetoed the whole project.

Interestingly, over the course of the next two years, easily 40 percent of the mid-to-senior management levels departed, as the impact of the newer executives, and their values, spread. In the opinion of most of those departing managers, the culture had changed so dramatically for the worse that they could no longer connect with the company and chose to move on.

This example reinforces the point that it's not just about who is recruited externally but also who is being promoted internally and where the talent management and development effort is going.

How can recruiting for values be incorporated into the recruitment process? As suggested in the chapter on implementation, part of the roll-out of the final stated values includes spending time identifying behaviors that upheld each of the values. Like a competency-based interview, these behaviors, along with other exercises (such as a values-ranking exercise, as outlined in chapter one, or evidence-based examples) could be incorporated into the recruitment process to determine how close a candidate's personal values relate to the company's.

Too many companies are sitting on a mound of potential that is never realized. Getting recruitment right is the difference between a mediocre, underperforming company and a company that harnesses their potential and turns it into real performance. As with anything, putting in the time and effort to get recruitment right at the beginning reaps huge rewards by allowing daily management focus on what it really should be focused on, not on managing poor performance and its negative impacts.

2. Company Values and Decision-Making

Returning to Joan and her values, following our original work, she was faced with a very difficult decision to make. Her industry was facing regulatory changes that were designed and being introduced, in Joan's opinion, due to vested interests. The expected impact on her business was to reduce the available distribution channels of her products.

She had researched many avenues, looking for ways to minimize the impact of the regulatory changes on her business. She finally identified a solution that potentially would not make her particularly popular with the powers-that-be but that would, strictly speaking, work within the regulations.

As Joan was updating me on this, I pointed out that she seemed comfortable with her decision and the possible outcomes. Her response was a very confident "yes." She went on to explain how she had used her values of freedom of choice, sustainability, and commercialism to guide her in making the right decision for her. Not only that, she was very happy with it and was already going full steam ahead, putting the plan into motion.

This is a great example of how using values can guide a decision and how more confident a person is in sensing or knowing that it is the right decision for them or the company. Not only does it seem "right," but the likelihood of the decision being implemented increases dramatically.

Unlike Joan, many people often make decisions in a void, separate from their values. Such decisions often result in an uncomfortable feeling or awareness that something is just not right with it. This niggling doubt, in turn, leads to self-doubt, questioning, discussing the issue with others, procrastination, and lack of action. They then beat themselves up over not getting things done and so the cycle continues.

In contrast, as we saw with Joan, a decision that honors the individual's values tends to sit well with them. There is less agonizing over whether it is the right decision or not. Their gut doesn't start sending out signals, nor do they need to discuss it ad nauseam or constantly revisit it. Not only that, because the decision seems so right to them, they act upon it and feel empowered by having seen progress and movement. In practice, things seem to just fall into place.

On an organizational basis, making decisions without regard to the company values leads to actions not matching words and employees sensing a disconnect, resulting in mistrust and conflict arising. If the company is saying that their set of values really is worthwhile and important to the company's long-term success, then it is important enough to be upheld, even during the decision-making process.

When decision-making is undertaken in a vacuum apart from the company values, a solution might be agreed on in theory, but in practice it is often not implemented, as it seems "wrong." There might not be an outright refusal to implement the proposal, but subtle sabotage might worm its way in or seemingly valid excuses keep being produced. In fact, as inaction follows inaction, the proposed solution is likely to be revisited numerous times before it is either dropped or altered.

In addition, when making decisions in times of crises, it is easy to forget what really is important and not take it into account. Instead, the "fight-or-flight" mechanism kicks in, making it harder to think with a clear head. Employees potentially make poor, ill-informed decisions and justify their actions after the fact. Such an approach to decision-making can result in all types of conflict and their associated costs.

To encourage a consistent application of values to decision-making, a discipline can be introduced throughout the company, so that consideration of the values and their impact on the final solution is consistently incorporated into the decision-making process. Such a discipline could be achieved by following the Living the Values Assessment (Practical Guide 5.3), adjusted for decision-making.

By taking the time to clearly understand what is and isn't important and in what order they are important in a period of calm, it becomes a lot easier to refer to and hold on to that framework in times of crisis or difficulty. Not only that, but, in retrospect, the proposed solution will most likely be the right one, reducing the need for twenty/twenty hindsight. This approach results in clear-headed decisions made with the company's best interests at heart.

3. Company Values and Marketing and Branding

In my simple way of looking to connect ideas and processes together, I see branding as the external promise to the market while the customer's interaction with the company informs their experience of whether the company delivers on the promise or not, as depicted in Diagram 7.1: Branding and Values.

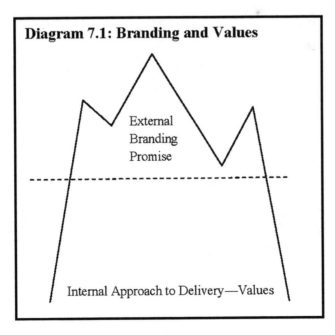

Diagram 7.1: Branding and Values

External Branding Promise

Internal Approach to Delivery—Values

This translates into the need for a clear and concrete connection between what is being promised (external to the organization) and what is being delivered (internal to the organization). Promising the earth and delivering a bucket of muck just doesn't sit well with most customers, encouraging them to depart in droves.

So, while the marketing director shouldn't be tasked with identifying a company's values, as per our earlier example, marketing, along with sales, does need to have a keen understanding of what makes this company different, as compared to how all its competitors approach the marketplace. Likewise, other departments need to have a keen awareness of the company's branding promise and how they can consistently deliver on that promise. This, inevitably, brings us back to the company values and how they link the two. Take Google[15], their brand and values. Their brand promise is to be innovative and, given that Google is relentless in its pursuit of exploring how we use and interact with the Internet, it's fair to say that, for the most part, consumer experience tallies with the promise of innovation. In some cases, consumers are probably just getting their heads around some of the functionality by the time the next wave of innovation hits.

Google's values are defined as "Ten Things We Know to Be True" and include such ideas as:

— Focus on the user and all else with follow.
— It's best to do one thing really, really well.
— You can make money without doing evil.

Given what is generally known about Google, in their approach to recruitment, workspace design, motivation, fostering creativity, user experience, censorship, etc., to an external observer, it's fair to say that they do seem to actively uphold these ten things internally. So, their brand promise of innovation connects through to user experience of Google products and services.

Matching the two elements has contributed to Google's meteoric rise from a Silicon Valley start-up to a $187-billion business, as

---

15 Google, Our Philosophy, Ten Things We Know to be True http://www.google. com/about/corporate/company/tenthings.html

of March 2011, achieved in little over a decade. More importantly, by recruiting for their values, they have managed to hire people who connect through to "how" Google wants to do business. This has resulted in their being able to maintain a small-company feel in a global organization that employs over twenty thousand people.

Let's be clear here: it's not to say that everyone agrees with Google or that Google is for everyone. From Google's perspective, as demonstrated by their recruitment process, they don't even want everyone. They only want those people who believe or value the same core principles they do, i.e., they recruit people that connect with Google's way of doing things. It is not right or wrong. There may be other, as effective ways to achieve similar results. However, Google's way works for them and so they are happy to apply their standards relatively consistently. This enables the company to replicate and sustain itself, both externally, through the brand, and internally, through its culture.

Finally, returning to how values connect with a company's mission statement, the mission statement states the company's purpose along with the values, which give guidance as to the specific approach the company is taking to achieve that purpose. It is that specific approach that differentiates one company from another and allows clear marketing and branding messages to be created and communicated.

If there are twenty accountancy practices, how does a customer know which one is best for them? After all, each practice offers a similar set of services: bookkeeping, tax-filing, accounts preparation, auditing, etc. How does any customer know what makes each of them different and which one is best for them?

Being able to clearly articulate what makes this business different provides a competitive advantage. What is different is usually not the product or service but the way in which the company engages in and relates to its client base, i.e., the *how*.

In addition to understanding the company's approach or values, it also simplifies the processes of identifying target audiences, filtering prospects, etc. An accountancy practice that values conformity and preparedness is best suited to attracting clients that are in highly regulated industries that hold values such as consistency, safety, or reliability. They are unlikely to connect too well with clients working in creative industries that hold such values as originality, creativity, or curiosity.

By clearly identifying and understanding the company's values, its marketing and sales efforts can be tailored to a specific group of potential clients that are more inclined to resonant with the message. As well as that, when new clients do bite, their experience of the company will match their expectations, lessening the likelihood of disappointment, conflict, and perceived "difficult" clients.

4. Company Values and Performance Management

If recruitment is important in ensuring that new employees do not dilute the culture generated by the company values, then performance management is key to ensuring that current employees actively support it.

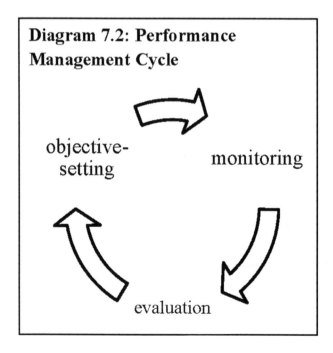

Diagram 7.2: Performance Management Cycle

objective-setting

monitoring

evaluation

As outlined in Diagram 7.2: Performance Management Cycle, the performance management cycle is typically made up of three stages:

— Objective-setting
— Monitoring
— Evaluation

During the objective-setting stage, two types of objectives need to be set: outcomes and behaviors.

Outcome objectives are those that clearly indicate "what" needs to be achieved. They are typically based on what the purpose of the job is. Several examples of outcome-based objectives include: an accountant preparing financial statements; a marketing executive creating a marketing strategy; a project manager delivering a project; an architect obtaining planning permission for a house.

Behavioral objectives are those that clearly indicate "how" employees should conduct themselves while performing their jobs and outcome objectives. For an in-depth example of a behavioral objective, see appendix D.

Best practice in performance evaluation recommends that evaluation is based on how well employees execute both their outcome and behavioral objectives. To achieve this, a weighting system should be applied to each type of objective, e.g., 50 percent for outcomes and 50 percent for behavioral, or 60 percent for outcomes and 40 percent for behavioral.

In reality, many companies don't have a formal and regular performance management process. For those that do, many set outcome objectives only. Of the companies that set both outcome and behavioral objectives, many either don't evaluate the behavioral objectives or they weight objectives in favor of the outcomes, i.e., 80 percent of the evaluation is given for outcomes while only 20 percent is given for behavioral objectives.

The impact of all this is that many performance management systems don't actively encourage and reward behavior; they only reward outcomes. A truism is that employees will do what they are rewarded for. So, if they are only rewarded for outcomes, they will deliver outcomes, regardless of behavior. If they are rewarded for outcomes and behaviors, then they will deliver outcomes and behaviors. In order to actively encourage employees to support the values, behavioral objectives should be set and performance evaluated on how well they achieved both their behavioral and outcome-based objectives.

5. Company Values and Leadership Development

The final section to incorporate values into is the area of leadership development. As we saw early on, being aware of and understanding one's personal values is a key element of developing one's ability to be an effective leader[16].

Self-Management

Personal values are drivers of a leader's thoughts, actions, and decisions, and they also actively influence a company's actual values and how those around them behave. Understanding their own values enables a leader to be aware of their emotional triggers. Such knowledge allows the leader to manage their emotions better, by not getting as frustrated, by de-personalizing situations, and by remaining level-headed, even in times of crisis.

Lack of understanding of personal values can result in a leader leaking emotion, behaving inconsistently, generating conflict, and potentially destroying trust with those around them. Such behaviors are neither in the interest of the leader or the company.

Conflict Management

As we have seen, conflict, be it intra-conflict or inter-conflict, triggers emotional responses, resulting in a leader not being able to think clearly, behave rationally, or hear what is really being said. Being aware of and understanding their personal values allows a

---

16 By "effective" leader, I mean someone with a vision that is able to inspire and influence others to achieve it, *not* someone who just happens to be in a senior position and has few leadership skills.

leader to spot times when they are behaving in a way inconsistent with them.

Relationship Management

Awareness of his or her own values also enables a leader to recognize when other people's behavior is at odds with their values. This allows leaders to retain the ability to see that it is not "personal," i.e., the other person is not "trying to get at us." In turn, this clarity of what is really taking place helps leaders to maintain perspective and better manage their emotions, their relationships, and their business.

Change Management

Understanding a leader's values can also shed light on their approach to change. The ability to enable change to happen and to lead employees toward implementing it is what being a leader is all about. After all, if nothing needed to change within a business, a good manager would suffice. A leader who values curiosity, discovery, spontaneity, fearlessness, creativity, originality, openness, learning, or knowledge is likely to be flexible and open to trying new ways or considering new ideas. Being open to new ideas is a key attribute of a successful leader.

In contrast, a leader who values order, control, certainty, safety, or security is likely to be quite inflexible because they want known outcomes and/or they want to minimize their exposure to risk. For such people, the thought of making a change or starting a process without knowing where it is going or having all the answers in advance often results in resistance to new ideas and change. For an employee in a leadership position, this is a weakness. Such a person might be a very effective senior manager but is unlikely to be an effective leader.

Emotional Intelligence

As outlined above, leaders who are aware of their personal values are better able to manage themselves, their relationships with others, conflict, and change, all of which are elements of emotional intelligence. Understanding one's own personal values is a key element in increasing self-awareness, which is a cornerstone of effective emotional intelligence. While many people feel that emotional intelligence is all about emotions and that the workplace is no place for emotions, the opposite is actually true. A person with a well-developed sense of who they are, what they are about, their strengths and weaknesses, and their feelings is less prone to becoming emotional in the workplace and more apt to remain calm and level-headed.

Values and Leadership Development

Any good leadership development program should include a personal values program, as outlined in Practical Guide 4.1, allowing the participants to identify their values, how they relate to the company values, and whether there are any obvious clashes. Ideally, the values program should be linked through to an emotional intelligence development section, with a cross-reference to their values to determine if any of them are causing low ability in a particular area that is key to leadership, e.g., change.

Revisiting the question of whether someone can change their values or not, for leaders who identify that their values are causing them some performance issues, these could then be addressed as part of a suitable executive coaching program. As part of their coaching, leaders can then determine if the cost of upholding the value outweighs or is outweighed by the benefits of adjusting, deranking, or changing it, and can make an informed decision as to what they want to do.

As we have seen, a leader whose personal values undermine a company's final stated value causes conflict and distraction, and hampers the company's ability to achieve its purpose. Leaders with personal values that naturally support the values are key to upholding them and turning the talk into action. They inspire those around them to do likewise, in turn promoting a harmonious workplace that enables the business to look forward and outwards, ensuring its long-term success.

Chapter Seven Summary

— *In order to sustain company values long-term, they need to be embedded into such processes as:*

  o *Recruitment*
  o *Decision-Making*
  o *Marketing and Branding*
  o *Performance Management*
  o *Leadership Development*

— **Recruitment:** *To prevent dilution, the values of new hires should complement the company's values. Promotions should only go to those that actively support the values. Recruit for compatible values, train for skills.*

— **Decision-Making:** *Decisions, company-wide, should be made using the company values, not by ignoring them.*

— **Marketing and Branding:** *Marketing and branding is the external promise to the customer while company values are the internal delivery on that promise. The marketing message should dovetail with the company's values.*

— **Performance Management:** *Two types of objectives should be set and evaluated: outcomes and behaviors.*

— **Leadership Development:** *Effective leaders are key to positioning an organization for future success. Effective leaders need personal values that naturally support final stated values, so that they consistently walk them, inspiring others to do likewise.*

Conclusion

While having lunch with a marketing executive, the subject of this book cropped up. I briefly outlined the concept and he started challenging me with questions such as: why are values necessary, how do they increase the bottom line, and lots of companies are successful on Wall St. without them, so why bother?

As each question was batted away, the conversation quickly moved to the nub of values: leadership. A company with strong leadership has a vision, a picture of what the company can achieve and what difference it will make when it is reality. Part of articulating that vision is to create a statement of intent that outlines both the purpose of the company and its approach to achieving it. These are otherwise known as the mission statement and values.

Companies don't *need* a vision, a mission statement, or values. They can bounce along quite nicely and be successful, even by Wall St.'s standards, but usually at a cost. Such costs include burn-out, turnover, loss of knowledge and skills, excessive use of resources, and loss of opportunities. Many of these companies are actually underperforming compared to what they *could* be doing. They are doing well enough but not compared to their capability. This is a huge, often unrecognized cost to a business.

Evidence shows that having a clear goal and a plan of how to achieve it mapped out increases successful outcomes. As we have seen, leading a business through a set of actively supported values creates a consistent, clear customer experience, building brand loyalty. It reduces conflict, freeing employees up to focus their energy on the business objectives rather than on the conflict. Company values also provide a framework and guidelines, within which employees have flexibility to execute their roles. In turn, this empowers employees to do their jobs, resulting in increased personal performance and underpinning increased team and company performance.

While clearly the implementation of an effective set of company values is not easy, the potential rewards far outweigh the initial pain. Company values really aren't just for the wall plaque; they provide a competitive advantage that drives the business forward.

APPENDIX A

Further Observations on Money

What is the impact of money on us? Clearly, we need money to live. When we don't have enough of it, it's a worry and puts us under pressure. When we have enough of it, we want more. For those who have more than they can ever spend, they declare it doesn't fulfill them. How can it impact us in so many different ways and do we actually value it in terms of personal values?

Take Marilyn, for example. During a conversation with her, she recounted how she was given a list of values to rank. When she ranked them the first time, money didn't feature. When she ranked them a second time several weeks later, money had moved up to tenth place. Typically, values don't move up or down so dramatically, so clearly something was going on for Marilyn in relation to money. Could it really be classed as a value, though?

Maslow's Theory of Needs:

To better understand the role money plays in our lives, I'm going to use a few different theories and tools, starting with Maslow's Hierarchy of Needs pyramid, as outlined in Figure A1.1.

For those of you who aren't acquainted with Maslow and his pyramid, let me give a quick explanation:

Basic Needs (survival):
First up is our need to meet our basic requirements, such as shelter, food, drink, and warmth. In the days of our ancestors, this meant finding a cave and some berries, killing a large enough animal to eat the meat and make clothes from the fur, and finding a clean source of water. In today's terms, it means having a roof over our heads, clothes, food, and drink, all of which is typically provided by either our parents/guardians or by getting out and supporting ourselves, i.e., making some money.

Figure A1.1: Maslow's Hierarchy of Needs Pyramid

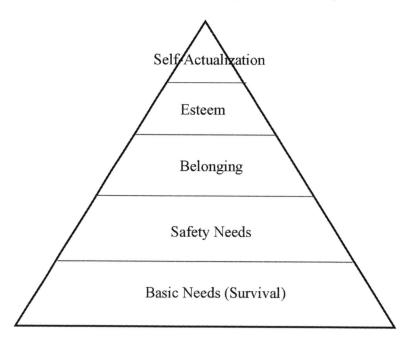

Safety Needs:

Once our basic needs are met, we start looking at the next level up, which deals with our safety. For example, if we've got a job that is providing enough to meet our basic needs, we start wanting to protect ourselves from losing those basic needs. We might start putting money into a pension or buy income protection or life insurance. We might want to find a more permanent home and so start looking to buy a house or apartment.

Belonging:

Next level up is the need to belong. This is where we've met enough of our needs that we have the energy to start worrying about being part of something. Being social animals, we want to connect with other people and feel part of something bigger than just ourselves. This is where an organization's culture starts to become important to us.

If we're still at levels one or two, we can't afford to worry about the culture, but once we're at level three, belonging and being part of something becomes increasingly important.

This observation is borne out by examining the behavior of graduates. In my experience, many graduates are so focused on getting a job that they are oblivious to an organization's culture. Its importance just doesn't register with them. However, as they gain some experience and meet their basic needs, they gradually start looking around them and wanting to be part of something. At this stage, if they don't like what they see, they move on and look for something more meaningful to them. This pattern is particularly prevalent in Generation Y graduates, that generation born in the 1980s and 1990s.

Esteem:

Next up is esteem, sometimes referred to as status. This level concerns itself with confidence, recognition, being respected, titles, and trophies, such as cars and homes.

Esteem is made up of two elements: respect and recognition from others, and self-respect.

Self-Actualization:

The tip of the pyramid is concerned with being the best a person can possibly be. It's about expanding horizons, trying out new things, creativity, and spontaneity. People at this level have already achieved success at all the other levels and sense there is something more to life, a higher purpose or untapped potential.

Several levels of Maslow's pyramid require some element of money. For example, money is needed to provide: shelter, food, heat, 401k contributions, cars, and material goods that indicate success. Both the belonging and self-actualization levels can be achieved without money but some elements may require money. For example, someone might need money to keep up with their peers in order to feel they belong while another person wouldn't. As for self-actualization, money might be necessary to allow a person to experience new horizons.

Moving Between Levels:

— Before a person can move up to the next level, they must have adequately met the requirements of the levels below it.
— Not everyone who reaches the esteem level will move into the self-actualization level.
— Life events can happen that move us down one or more levels, e.g., redundancy, loss of a loved one, a house fire.

Hertzberg's Two-Factor Theory of Motivation:

Hertzberg's Motivating-Hygiene Theory splits factors into two categories: hygiene factors and motivating factors. In a nutshell, his theory is that hygiene factors are factors that, once present, don't motivate but, if they aren't present, actively de-motivate. Motivating factors, on the other hand, do actively motivate people to improve performance and engage in the overall purpose of the team or organization.

An example of a hygiene factor is having basic resources such as a desk, computer, phone, paper, and printer (in the case of an office-based worker) or spades, shovels, diggers, concrete, and hammers (in the case of a builder).

The de-motivating impact of missing hygiene factors was never so acutely brought home to me as during one particular interview. The interviewee was a young man looking to change companies. Aside from the fact that the job market of the day was decidedly mobile and transient, I probed why he was looking to move. He explained that he had been in his current company for six months and he still didn't have his own work station, computer terminal, or any personal space. This was de-motivating him so much that, while he liked the work and the people, he just couldn't keep working with no designated base. The irony is, of course, that had he had those basics, he wouldn't have even noticed them, but not having them was dragging him down.

An example of a motivating factor is to be given more responsibility. One of my favorite stories comes from a manager I worked with several years ago. Brad had attended one of my management development programs, during which I had talked about the upward spiral of developing staff to be able to successfully complete their work, freeing up the team lead/manager's time to achieve other tasks, etc. I had also talked about the downward spiral of how always "just doing the task yourself" prevented people from developing, which never freed up the team lead/manager and, over time, gets progressively worse.

As it turned out, Brad was in such a downward spiral, to the point that the work had completely skewed away from the junior staff and was placed firmly in the laps of the supervisors, assistant manager, and Brad himself. Recognizing that his situation was never going to change if he didn't do something different, he bit the bullet, sat down with his management team, and figured out a plan to get back onto the upward spiral.

About four or five months later, I met Brad in the corridor and asked him how things were going. Knowing the bad space he and his team had been in, I was very taken aback when he responded, "Brilliant! We're meeting all our deadlines, I've loads more time, and things couldn't be better." I inquired if this included being able to spare the time to give a thirty-minute talk about his experience at my next management development program. It did.

At the next session, Brad joined us and shared his story with the group. He outlined how most of the work had crept its way onto the supervisors and AMs' desks, how the staff had been doing what they could but were leaving at 5:00 p.m. every day, how he and the supervisors/AMs worked fourteen-hour days two out of every four weeks, how they were constantly missing their deadlines, how upset the client was, how poor the quality of their work was, and the additional stress this put them under. It really was a nasty picture. We all felt for Brad.

Then he started to talk about how he had attended the training program and how it finally dawned on him that it couldn't continue. So, he sat down with his management team and started planning their approach. They divvied up the work, drew up training plans for each staff member on all the different tasks, and, in three months, they had completely turned the situation around. The participants were mesmerized at this stage, firing questions at him.

The one thing that amused me the most was Brad's sheer astonishment at how much more motivated his junior staff was. He had feared that they would resent being asked to do their job or they wouldn't want to help out but the reality was they were delighted to take on more responsibility and accountability. Most likely, they had been sitting there, bored stupid every day, and here was a great opportunity to (a) do something and make the day go faster, (b) learn and understand what they were supposed to be doing, and (c) possibly even start dreaming of moving up the ladder (it was a very fast-paced environment where people with any ability were promoted quickly). They grasped the chance to take on more responsibility with both hands and neither Brad nor his team looked back.

Having looked at the difference between hygiene and motivating factors, Hertzberg's theory places money as straddling both sets of factors, with a bias towards the hygiene. To put this into simpler words, this indicates that:

— Not having enough money to cover the basics of life is de-motivating.
— Once the basics are consistently met, a certain amount of additional money will motivate.
— At some tipping point, other motivating factors will become more important, outweighing the power of using money as a motivator.

The "tipping point" or level of money required for any given individual depends on the individual. For some, it will be once their basic needs and some of their comforts are met. For others, it will be once they have enough to realize some of their dreams. If money can be a value, it is more likely to be a positional value. If a person doesn't have enough, it becomes significant. If they have enough to meet a reasonable amount of their expectations, its importance fades away.

Needs, Wants, and Wishes Analysis

One exercise that can shed light on where a person's tipping point might be in relation to money is the Needs/Wants/Wishes exercise.

A Needs/Wants/Wishes[17] form splits a page into four columns: Area of Need, Needs, Wants, and Wishes. Under the column of Area of Need, the individual writes in the area of consideration. Under each subsequent column, the individual jots down the differing levels they require to meet that need. See Table AA.1 for an example:

---

17 See www.irialofarrell.com to download blank Needs/Wants/Wishes forms.

Table AA.1
Example of Needs/Wants/Wishes

Area	Need	Want	Wish
Transport	To get from A to B, using public transport or a bike	A car to get me from A to B	A BMW
Shelter	Somewhere to live but not in parental home, e.g., rented	To rent an apartment with just one other person	To own my own home
Love	To have interactions with people, including hugs	To be in an intimate relationship	To find my soulmate

Connecting the Theory Back to Money:

Relating the Needs/Wants/Wishes tool back to both Maslow's and Hertzberg's theories and connecting it to our need for money, it's fair to say that we need to have enough money available to meet all our requirements under the Needs column. If we don't, the lack of money to meet those needs will most likely lead to a de-motivating effect.

Once the basic needs are met, we can start fulfilling our wants, as outlined in the Wants column, and earning excess money to meet these can be very motivating. So, earning an additional two thousand or five thousand dollars a year, when we're focused at this level, can act as a motivator as it allows us to start moving into the esteem area, assuming that we have already met our need to belong, i.e., we connect with and have built positive relationships with our co-workers.

At some point, between meeting most of the requirements in the Wants column and starting to move into the Wishes column, money as a motivator starts to diminish and other things, such as title, status, respect and/or achievement, become more important. At this point, the tipping value of "money" has been reached.

Again, for some people, it is well worth taking the time to explore and understand what money does represent to them. As I said, I've never encountered someone who explicitly states money as a value but, if someone does feel they value it, it might be that they value it as an enabler or as a representative of something else, such as power, choice, or altruism.

For such people, an interesting exercise might be for them to consider how they prioritize their money. As money tends to be a limited resource, taking time to consider their thought process in determining how they use it will give them further insight into what is of value or importance to them.

APPENDIX B

Values and Competency Frameworks

Readers acquainted with competency frameworks might be wondering if values are the same as behavioral competencies. As such, no, they are not the same, although they should work in conjunction with each other.

A competency framework is a set of behaviors that, if captured correctly, typically defines the expected or acceptable actions within the organization. They are usually clustered into groups such as communication, results-focus, people management, project management, self-management, etc., and each cluster is referred to as a "competency." Each competency may or may not also include an expected goal for each level within the organizational structure. See Table AB.1: Example of a Competency Framework for a better understanding of a competency and its behavioral indicators:

Table AB.1
Example of a Competency Framework

Competency	Communication		
Level	1	2	3
Goal	To ensure that information is clearly delivered to others	To ensure that people are kept informed	To analyze information, make decisions, and notify relevant parties
Behavioral Indicators	– Written material is concise and clear – Information is delivered in a timely manner	– To determine who needs to know what – To ensure relevant people are notified	– Analyze information – Draw conclusions and options – Determine course of action – Notify relevant parties

APPENDIX C

Detailed Approach to Conducting the Values Workshop

1. Prior to holding a values workshop, I asked the ten or so executives to identify five to eight values that they felt were important for the company and to forward them to me.
2. Based on how regularly a suggested value turned up, I compiled a short list of six possible values and these became the basis of our workshop.
3. In the workshop, each executive defined what each of the six values meant to them.
4. The definitions were pooled and a final definition for each short-listed value was agreed upon.
5. I then asked them to rank the list, one to six, in order of how important they saw them, considering the company's future needs.
6. I then asked them to rate each value, using a scale of one to five, to indicate how alive they felt each value was in the current environment.

7. Once I compiled the numbers, I plotted them as shown in Diagram AC.1: Plotted Values, and named the quadrants as follows:

   ○ Valid values (actual values to be retained)
   ○ Missing values (values needed that didn't currently exist)
   ○ Comfort values (actual values to be dumped)
   ○ Red herrings (values discussed but not seen as either important or alive)

Diagram AC.1: Plotted Values

	Alive	**Not Alive**
Important	*Valid*	*Missing*
Not Important	*Comfort*	*Red Herrings*

This process allowed the group to identify the current actual values (valid and comfort values), the missing values, and the required final stated values (valid plus missing values). By following this process, the executive team had defined the meanings of each value, identified the actual values, undertaken a values gap analysis, highlighted missing values, and agreed on a set of final stated values.

APPENDIX D

Example of a Behavioral Objective

A behavioral objective is an objective designed to change an observable behavior or to develop it. Using the level 3 behavioral indicators for communication, as described in Table AB.1 in appendix B, an example of a behavioral indicator is as follows:

Currently, the employee goes to the manager with all the information with the expectation that the manager will make the decision and notify the relevant parties. This behavior needs to change so the manager is going to set a behavioral objective:

Step 1: For the next x days or weeks, rather than coming with all the information, the employee is to read the data, assess it, and consider what they would do, then bring it to the manager and explain the data and how they are interpreting it.

Step 2: As the employee is explaining, the manager may ask some questions to ensure they have considered all aspects of the data. Initially, the manager makes the decision but, over time, the employee puts forward the decision they would make. At the end of each such interaction, the manager asks questions to ensure the employee fully understands the reasons the final decision was made.

Step 3: As the employee's confidence builds up, the next step is for the employee to analyze the data, identify two or three potential solutions, and isolate their preferred decision. They then present this to the manager, answering any questions the manager may have in relation to the data or the analysis. Over time, this builds up both the employee and the manager's confidence in the employee's decision-making abilities.

Step 4: As further confidence builds, the employee analyzes the data, and presents both their proposed decision and their list of who needs to be notified to the manager. Once the manager is happy that the employee is consistently capable of making the right decisions and identifying the right people to notify, the employee is freed up to run with their own decision-making.

As we can see, by the end of the objective, the employee is competent to analyze data, make accurate decisions off the back of the analysis, and correctly identify who needs to be notified of such decisions, all with the backing and confidence of the manager.

WORKS CITED

Jim Collins, *Good to Great* (Random House, 2001), "Chapter Two: Level 5 Leadership" and "Chapter Four: Confront the Brutal Facts"

Michael Lewis, *The Big Short* (Penguin, 2010), page 86

Ludwig Report, available from AIB Group website, http://www.aibgroup.com/servlet/BlobServer/document.pdf?blobkey=id&blobwhere=1015597173380&blobcol=urlfile&blobtable=AIB Download&blobheader=application/pdf&blobheadername1=Content-Disposition&blobheadervalue1=document.pdf, pages 15 and 17

Robin Sharma, *The Monk Who Sold His Ferrari* (Element, 2004), page 134

Jack Welch with Suzy Welch, *Winning* (HarperCollins, 2005), page 20-21

GLOSSARY

401k Contribution
Personal pension contributions made by US citizens. Term refers to the relevant subsection of the US Internal Revenue Code

Behavioral Indicators
Statements that describe a specific set of observable behaviors

Behavioral Objectives (how)
Objectives set to develop or change a person's observable behavior in how they perform their job

CEO
Chief executive officer, the head of the company

CFO
Chief financial officer, the person in charge of the company's finances

Competency Framework
A framework that highlights the areas employees at different levels within the organization need to be competent in. Many of the areas tend to be based on skills and abilities rather than technical knowledge. The framework is often accompanied by behavioral indicators to further explain the competencies.

Company, Core, Corporate Values
All different terms used to describe values used within an organization

CSR
Customer service representative, a term used to describe an employee working in front-line customer service

CYA
Cover your ass—a term used to describe actions taken by an individual to ensure blame is not apportioned to them

Organizational Design (OD)
Any work undertaken within an organization to align structures, processes and rewards with its strategy and purpose

Outcome Objectives (what)
Objectives based on results the employee needs to achieve. They tend to be tangible, may be project-based or ongoing, and are usually closely aligned with their job.

Outliers
A statistical term used to indicate that isolated results that were far away from the main cluster of results were left out

Performance Evaluation
A term used to indicate the meeting at the end of a performance cycle, with the purpose of looking back on the period and determining how well the employee performed

Performance Management System
A term used to describe the combination of all the stages of performance, including all accompanying procedures and forms

Recruitment Process
A term used to describe a company's approach to recruitment, both internal and external, and includes policies, forms, procedures, promotions, etc.

Shared Technology Platform
Refers to any IT system that allows multiple users to safely access the same on-line space and engage in on-line dialogues in real time

Survey Bias
During the construction phase of a survey, questions that lead respondents to specific answers, limit their options, or confuse can lead to results that are misrepresentative. In particular, they might give the desired answers rather than the real answers.

Talent Management
A term used to describe the process of attracting and retaining top performers. This can include elements of the recruitment process as well as employee development such as a leadership development program and job rotation.

ABOUT THE AUTHOR

Irial is fascinated by how people behave and perform in companies, what contributes to employees reaching the required standard of performance, and what derails others. Since her first office-based job in Sydney, Australia, she's been fascinated by the traits, characteristics, and abilities of good managers and leaders and how they can inspire and compel employees to go the extra mile.

She is driven by helping and enabling people to develop and reach their potential within business. This has led Irial on her own personal journey from doing the work to managing the team that did the work to developing the managers who managed the teams that did the work to coaching the leaders who run the companies, so that everyone can succeed. This journey led her to leadership and how it works in practice. By studying areas such as philosophy, business, coaching, training, leadership, and emotional intelligence, she has gained deep insight into what is required to cultivate and develop effective leadership. This includes assessing the various theories and simplifying them into common themes, enabling leaders to clearly understand and apply the core fundamentals of leadership at both the personal and organizational levels, rather than getting confused by all the theory.

Irial works with individuals and teams in the areas of personal values, company values, leadership development, emotional intelligence, and executive coaching.

For more information about Irial and the services she provides, please visit www.irialofarrell.com or www.evolutionconsulting.ie.

12437728R00111

Made in the USA
Charleston, SC
05 May 2012